MW00423199

"A clear and practical guidebook on the personal tools necessary for leadership success, *Lead the Way in Five Minutes a Day* provides a blueprint for achieving excellence in leadership in today's challenging professional environment. Jo Anne Preston presents a path forward for aspiring leaders and seasoned executives alike who wish to improve their skills."

—Alan Morgan, CEO, National Rural Health Association

"Jo Anne Preston's wisdom has guided me for years and will likely shape my development for years to come. With so many leadership books to choose from, this one should be at the top of the list! Jo's sincere, thoughtful approach to healthcare leadership synthesizes complex, often overwhelming, aspects of leading teams into an easy-to-consume and easy-to-implement format that will empower and encourage any leader, no matter where they are on their leadership journey."

—Angelina Salazar, CEO, Western Healthcare Alliance

"Leadership competence is one of the top skills needed in a fast-changing world. *Lead the Way in Five Minutes a Day* speaks to the need for leadership to be able to listen, learn, and understand both the circumstances and the context of emerging trends and issues. In it, Jo Anne Preston describes her leadership experiences—the good, the bad, and the lessons learned. She provides work tools for personal and team approaches to executing leadership, solving complex problems, and envisioning the future. The book is a culmination of her experience, spirit, and wisdom. It is a remarkable mixture of practical information and human values. Without a doubt, it is a view of leadership worth reading."

—Barbara Nichols, executive director,
Wisconsin Center for Nursing

PRAISE FOR
LEAD THE WAY IN FIVE MINUTES A DAY

"I've had the good fortune of working with Jo Anne Preston for the past several decades and have observed her extraordinary ability to engage and inspire nurses and department managers in her workshops. *Lead the Way in Five Minutes a Day* gathers some of the key nuggets of wisdom from Jo's workshops. I highly recommend this book to anyone working in healthcare."

—Terry Hill, senior advisor for rural health leadership and policy, National Rural Health Resource Center, and executive director, Rural Health Innovations

"Do I see myself? Do I see opportunities for growth? Is this what I need now? These questions echo three truths shared by Jo Anne Preston in the conclusion of her book, *Lead the Way in Five Minutes a Day*. The answer to each is yes. This book is a well-organized tool that demands self-reflection and action using a clever self-assessment scoring technique. As the title suggests, by referring to it regularly I can use it to identify and act on leadership opportunities in real-time."

—John T. Supplitt, senior director of field engagement, Rural Health Services, American Hospital Association

"Over the years, I've read many books intended to help leaders, in healthcare and beyond, get better at what they do. Authors can easily evangelize for *their* way. That's not Jo Anne Preston. With her concise, evidence-based leadership ideas, she has always struck me as an insightful collaborator who is as aware of my unique circumstances as her own. Because *leadership matters,* I enthusiastically recommend this book. Take Jo on your unique journey, as she welcomes you on hers."

—A. Clinton MacKinney, MD, MS, clinical associate professor, College of Public Health, University of Iowa

LEAD THE WAY IN FIVE MINUTES A DAY

LEAD THE WAY IN FIVE MINUTES A DAY

Sparking High Performance in Yourself and Your Team

JO ANNE PRESTON

ACHE Management Series

Your board, staff, or clients may also benefit from this book's insight. For information on quantity discounts, contact the Health Administration Press Marketing Manager at (312) 424-9450.

Library of Congress Cataloging-in-Publication Data

Names: Preston, Jo Anne, author.
Title: Lead the way in five minutes a day : sparking high performance in yourself and your
  team / Jo Anne Preston.
Description: Chicago, IL : Health Administration Press, [2021] | Series: HAP/ACHE
  management series | Includes bibliographical references. | Summary: "This book is
  an easy-to-use resource that zeroes in on a leader's real-life struggles and offers clear
  solutions—without complex theory or jargon. The reader will learn tips that can be applied
  immediately and discover practical actions for improving skills. Although the book can be
  read from cover to cover, it is organized by topic to allow for a stand-alone, five-minute
  read of leadership tips, reflections, and suggestions"—Provided by publisher.
Identifiers: LCCN 2020042441 (print) | LCCN 2020042442 (ebook) | ISBN 9781640552357
  (paperback) | ISBN 9781640552326 (epub) | ISBN 9781640552333 (mobi)
Subjects: LCSH: Leadership.
Classification: LCC HD57.7 .P744 2021 (print) | LCC HD57.7 (ebook) | DDC
  658.4/092—dc23
LC record available at https://lccn.loc.gov/2020042441
LC ebook record available at https://lccn.loc.gov/2020042442

The paper used in this publication meets the minimum requirements of American National Standard for Information Sciences—Permanence of Paper for Printed Library Materials, ANSI Z39.48-1984. ⊗ ™

Acquisitions editors: Janet Davis and Jennette McClain; Manuscript editor: Deborah Ring; Project manager: Andrew Baumann; Layout: Integra

Found an error or a typo? We want to know! Please e-mail it to hapbooks@ache.org, mentioning the book's title and putting "Book Error" in the subject line.

For photocopying and copyright information, please contact Copyright Clearance Center at www.copyright.com or at (978) 750-8400.

Health Administration Press
A division of the Foundation of the American
  College of Healthcare Executives
300 S. Riverside Plaza, Suite 1900
Chicago, IL 60606-6698
(312) 424-2800

This book is dedicated to the people who have allowed me the privilege to lead while I was still learning. I hope you survived my steep curve and surpassed me.

Contents

Foreword

I FIRST MET Jo Preston on a cold, rainy, snow-melting day in Sauk City, Wisconsin, where three of us had come to pitch a program to her. My colleagues, a Zen teacher and a physician, were also faculty members of the Department of Family Medicine at the University of Wisconsin, and I head the Institute for Zen Leadership (IZL). Together, we had developed the HEAL (Healthy Embodied Agile Leadership) program for healthcare leaders and practitioners. The Rural Wisconsin Health Cooperative (RWHC) had invited us to talk about the program and see whether HEAL was right for the communities it serves. Jo was senior manager for workforce and organizational development at RWHC. Having taught countless leadership programs herself, she might have felt threatened by a new program like ours.

Jo was just the opposite. She lit up as we described what we were doing—bringing deep, physical practices into leadership development—and signed up for the next program we offered. One might think that with her decades of experience, she would have come to our program with a full cup. Not so. She soaked up everything with thirstiness and grace, and when she spoke, it was for the sake of others: perfectly timed, perfectly tuned.

Jo embodies how to lead the Way, which is not only a good title for a book, but also a tagline for IZL. It speaks not only to carving a way forward for others but also to sensing the bigger picture, the larger forces at work, and leading attuned to all of it. When we can get out of our own way, we naturally resonate with *the* Way, which is not a paved road so much as an ongoing process of listening deeply and steering skillfully.

These are exactly the forces that shaped this book and what it can do for you. It was deep listening to the needs of her colleagues that informed Jo's monthly column year after year. It was hearing from grateful newly promoted managers, experienced senior administrators, physicians, and others who had used her practical advice that prompted Jo to assemble her years of writing into a book. It is to help you skillfully steer your day that Jo serves up this book in such an accessible, digestible form.

This is the kind of book that could only come from decades of leadership and teaching experience. As you read it, you can almost feel how Jo learned this lesson, or applied that one, or crafted this set of learnings into a module that she had taught so many times she could distill the essence. You can also feel how she wrote this for you, how she wants you to succeed past the limits of the weakest aspects—real or imagined—of your leadership.

This book is also highly efficient, organized according to a set of reflections at the beginning of each chapter that help you discern which lessons will be most helpful to you *now*. Flip to that section, and in just a few minutes, you can zero in on something to remember or practice today. In the first chapter, for example, I felt a buzz of recognition when I came to the self-assessment question about overapologizing, and I knew that was a section I needed to read. Sure enough, I came away with the useful "Goldilocks rule." It took less than five minutes.

That is not to say that you have to read this book in a hurry, or spin yourself into a state of perpetual rush, which talk of "minutes" can move us to do. As a Zen teacher, what I appreciate about the tiny moments in which this book can be digested is that they are conducive to *practice*. Daily practice. In-your-life practice. A bit of just-in-time wisdom that you can put into practice in the next conversation you have or the next meeting you attend. A tip here, a practice there, and over time, you get a feel for the boundless wisdom of leading the Way.

This book is a gift. Enjoy it and use it well!

—Ginny Jiko Whitelaw

Preface

"I'm going to school to become a . . ." Maybe, maybe not. In fact, very few people I know ended up working in precisely the job they imagined when they began preparing for their career. My plan didn't include working in the substance abuse treatment and prevention field, but I spent about 20 years there. No matter what job I would have started with, I always aspired to leadership. My experiences as I moved up through the ranks in behavioral healthcare provided a rich training ground for the second half of my four-decade career coaching and teaching leaders.

It is interesting and sometimes surprising to me as I teach leaders how often the relevance of my work in behavioral healthcare connects to the development of all kinds of leaders. In my experience, these areas of my work intersect in three significant and meaningful ways:

1. **Leaders who share their struggles with peers learn from each other and benefit from that support.** I teach workshops covering a wide range of leadership topics to healthcare leaders, particularly those who have recently been promoted. I often announce to the participants that our classroom is our support group, and I encourage people to take advantage of it. These are the people who "get" you and remind you that you are not alone in your struggles—that we must lean on each other. This feeling of belonging is a big reason support groups work. We need

each other. Thinking we can do leadership on our own is a recipe for burnout.

2. **We are most successful when we keep things simple.** This is not to say that leadership—or life, for that matter—is easy. And I am not suggesting we ignore the complexities and messiness of life. But there is beauty and wisdom in drilling down to the fundamentals, which can help us get through challenges. Simple messages keep the focus on what you can control. They come in handy when we start trying to do too much at once, worrying too much about the future, or finding fault with others rather than accepting personal accountability. Instantly, we can shift the way we see ourselves. Many days, we must simply show up and begin. The little things we remind ourselves to do or say can make all the difference in how effectively we do that.

3. **Trust makes all the difference, and it starts with trusting yourself.** Trust yourself to do the best you can, to never stop learning, and to stay humble. Trust yourself to stay open and willing to learn even when you think you have it all figured out. Trust that every challenge is an opportunity rather than a setback or failure.

Mentoring has always mattered to me. Initially, I wanted to be a counselor. That desire took a variety of forms throughout my career: therapist, employee assistance counselor, prevention specialist, executive director, organizational development consultant, coach, teacher, and manager. No matter the job title, nothing has been more satisfying in my work than seeing someone I have coached become their best self.

One of my first jobs, working with teens in peer leadership programs, brought this to light for me. These teens gathered in a facilitated environment to support positive decision-making, particularly about alcohol and other drugs, but also about healthy choices in general. These programs aimed to encourage young people to develop leadership skills and to bring others along with them to make healthy choices—a positive peer pressure of sorts—all with the support of caring adults. I was one of those caring adults, and I still am. My audience has shifted from teens to adults, but the key principle remains the same: Know that you make a difference, and do your best to make the difference that you alone can make.

Another pivotal experience occurred about three months into my first professional job as a youth counselor, when I was asked whether I would like to supervise the people I worked with. It was flattering to be promoted so quickly. I distinctly remember thinking, "How hard can this be?" Very hard, as it turns out. Being good at leading and managing is a whole different skill set than succeeding in the job we're promoted from.

Like many leaders, I learned a lot of things through trial and error. You may relate to some of my learning experiences. I have had to:

- Fire a good friend
- Get myself out of the middle of others' conflicts (which I erroneously thought they needed me to solve)
- Address bad behavior that I had ignored, hoping it would magically go away (spoiler alert: it didn't)
- Lose out on opportunities because I waited too long to make a decision
- Correct the fallout from a decision when I acted too quickly
- Admit that I should have asked for help sooner to avoid a calamity

I have gotten some things right, too. For instance, I have been known to:

- Navigate the move from peer or friend to manager successfully
- Facilitate positive turnarounds in work culture

- Address and correct underperformance
- Share just the right wisdom or coaching question at the moment it was needed
- Attract and appreciate a diverse team
- Admit when I was wrong and fix it

This book originated from a desire to take those lessons—the good and the bad—and create a practical, skill-based, self-reflective, and actionable resource for leaders. Having worked with busy healthcare professionals for my whole career, I wanted to give new and experienced leaders a resource that they could grab onto and work with quickly, so I began writing a monthly one-page leadership newsletter in 2010. Every month, the topics were informed by listening to what was on the minds of other leaders and drawing on my own experiences.

Many of those newsletters are now collected and organized into sections of this book. I did not start out with a grand plan for a book about what leaders need to know; I credit the leaders who shared their struggles with me for creating the topics for this collection. Each topic was written to be read in about five minutes. While it is based on theory and years of experience, this writing is not theory. My hope is that on any given day, you can find just what you need and carry it with you as your approach your work today and in the future.

Acknowledgments

PREPARING TO WRITE this section has been an exercise in looking to the past for all the good. In the process I even remembered my fifth-grade teacher from a half century ago, Mrs. Morgan. She knew that I liked to write poems and that my family didn't have money for extra school supplies, so she bought me my own special notebook to use for writing poems and stories. *Teachers: Whatever form your "classroom" takes, you matter forever in our lives.* This memory brought me to my first realization about writing this acknowledgments section, which is that a page limit would be impossible because I am fortunate to have been surrounded by this kind of greatness all of my life.

The second realization was that the contributions to this book specifically recognized here are a continuation of its contents: examples of leadership. So I invite you to view my gratitude list as a set of bonus leadership tips from those who have made a difference to me and who contributed significantly to the creation of this book.

There are many who are unnamed here, but you have my gratitude nonetheless. If we have had a conversation, a shared classroom experience, a work history, a management relationship, or a friendship, I have learned something from you, and you are here in these pages. I believe each of us is like a tapestry whose threads are woven from the connections we make with each other. All of the threads, even the tiny ones, have a place in the piece of art. You are part of my art. And of course, as you read this book, I weave my way into yours. *Leaders: Realize that you actually become a part of the people you interact with—every person, every time. It's a big responsibility, and like Mrs. Morgan's impact on me, it can be long lasting.*

I am grateful to my extraordinary employer, the Rural Wisconsin Health Cooperative, for being a phenomenal place to grow, create, and thrive. A few people I specifically mention here include our unstoppable executive director, Tim Size, and my manager, Darrell Statz, for their boundless support and nearly embarrassing levels of recognition. Chris Brown, you have always made my monthly newsletters look amazing with your art and design skills. My department colleagues Cella Janisch Hartline, Erin Smital, and Carrie Ballweg are a dream team. How lucky I am to have such talented coworkers who tell each other "I love you" and mean it. *Leaders: Hone your values, then create a positive work culture by exhibiting those values in your daily behaviors. Recognize people who align to those values, and you will never have to address productivity.*

Thank you, Dr. Clinton MacKinney, for repeatedly responding to my leadership newsletters over the years by urging me to collect them into this book, for seeing the possibilities before I could, and ultimately for forging the connection with Health Administration Press to publish it. *Leaders: Be a nudge for others' success, and be a connector to ease the path.*

Thank you, Janet Davis; you took this project into your hands, delivered it with care to reviewers and decision makers, and made the case for this book to be in the reader's hands right now. *Leaders: Know that the work others deliver to you has their heart in it, and handle it accordingly.*

Thank you, Deb Knippel, dear friend and personal librarian, for researching a thousand copyright questions and for actually being interested in doing so. Thank you, as well, for veering off into knitting conversations with me from time to time. *Leaders: Show interest, go the extra mile, and know that sometimes it pays off to just take a break.*

Thank you, Jaci Griffin, for "cleaning the house before the housecleaner came" by providing an initial review. This is my first book, and your full read from start to finish, with all of your suggestions, helped me to feel more confident when I sent it off to the publisher. *Leaders: Be willing to ask for, and graciously receive, help.*

The surprisingly fun part of this project (once I picked myself up off the floor after seeing the high number of changes) was editing. Deb Ring, you really cleaned all the corners, made me sound smarter than I am, and corrected me in such a way that I was genuinely sad when the editing was done. I may write another book just so I can experience that again. *Leaders: Sometimes you have to tell people they are wrong, and it can stir up defensiveness. How you correct someone makes a big difference. It helps to make it a dialogue, keep the focus on the desired end goal, share your reasoning, offer alternatives, and be clear about who makes the final decision.*

I am grateful to the others at Health Administration Press for their belief in this project, particularly Andrew Baumann, who put up with my endless questions and stayed professional while helping me to remember not to take it all too seriously. *Leaders: Sometimes you have to take a chance on someone, and once you decide to take that chance, be all in. A sense of humor doesn't hurt either.*

This book has come together during the same time frame that I have been training in Zen leadership. It is no accident that these two experiences are in sync. The embodiment of leadership is something I work on daily now. Ginny Whitelaw, thank you for showing up in my life. I didn't even know to wish for you, and there you were, bringing along with you so many new friendships and a support network from all over the globe through your powerful teaching. *Leaders: Invite yourself into spaces you might not otherwise go. Put your whole body into learning, especially when you think you have it figured out in your head.*

I thank my first team, "team Griffin": Alice, Mike, Becky, David, Dan, Jim, Tom, and Rob, and our first coaches/managers, Mom and Dad. This perfectly imperfect group continues to teach me lessons in teamwork, diversity, conflict, trust, and how to share nicely. *Leaders: Teams can be messy sometimes, but everyone has a unique and valuable gift to offer. When you get a team to commit, it can overcome just about anything.*

Finally, I thank my home team, Mike, for reminding me to stop and appreciate moments that I might have missed because I am not paying attention, especially those in the natural world: the buds of growth on spring trees, the mama deer and nursing fawn that haven't detected our human presence, the "stories" in the snow from the night's activity in the winter woods. You keep my feet on the ground while my head is dreaming, and this is the fertile soil for my best ideas. I thank you also for our daughters, Hannah and Kelsey, who fill my heart with love and have taught me to forgive myself for my mistakes. *Leaders: Be that person who reminds others to pause and enjoy the present, to let go and forgive the past, and to keep moving forward. Love what matters, for love is what matters.*

Introduction

Suzanne Clark, president of the U.S. Chamber of Commerce, was interviewed in an April 14, 2020, segment on PBS's *NewsHour* titled "The New Challenges Businesses May Face in a World Changed by COVID-19." A month earlier, the country had ground to a halt economically so that people could stay safe at home. Speaking about how to get the economy back up and running again, Clark admitted, "There is no playbook to take off the shelf and execute." No kidding. The novel coronavirus has been a crisis like none other we have experienced.

There is, however, a playbook for leadership. Leading is less about what you are up against and more about what you bring to the table. While you can't prepare for every situation, you can prepare yourself to lead. That is what you will find in the pages ahead.

This book is for you if you want to:

- Learn leadership tips that you can apply immediately.
- Glean insights from research but don't have the time to read long theoretical books.
- Grab onto practical actions for getting better at difficult skills. Most people call them soft skills, but I don't. They are hard—just ask anyone who has ever had to address a personal hygiene issue with an employee, collaborate on a project with an undermining colleague, or manage a conflict between two angry coworkers who refuse to work together.

This book is also for you if you are:

- New to a leadership role.
- Aspiring to be in a leadership role.
- Experienced as a leader but are entering a new position. A new environment is an opportunity to reflect on where you are now compared with where you were in your past role as a leader.
- Ready to lead some days, but on other days, you reluctantly step to the front when at least some part of you would rather hold back. There is something here for the hesitant leader, too.

HOW TO USE THIS BOOK

While you certainly may read this book from cover to cover, it is meant to be more like a reference book. You can go to the topic you need today for a stand-alone, five-minute read containing tips, reflections, actions to take, and techniques for addressing whatever challenge you are facing in the moment.

This book consists of 11 chapters that focus on topics that leaders think about or need to address almost daily:

1. **Communication.** Not surprisingly, this is the biggest chapter. While just about anything could fall under this heading, here you will find help with getting your point across effectively in the unique situations that leaders face. Your communication is your superpower. The topics here guide you in becoming intentional and impactful.

2. **Inspiration.** Some days you just need a spark to keep yourself and others excited about growth and learning. Look here to find fuel for your vision of success and pearls of wisdom to guide you to it.

3. **Work Habits.** Our daily actions add up over time to make us effective—or not. Building habits that refuel you and direct your energy to the right effort will pay off and prevent burnout and becoming overwhelmed.

4. **Performance Evaluations.** Make them meaningful and worthwhile, not meaningless and a waste of time. Learn in this section about biases, ratings, and skills to turn this process into a motivator.

5. **Teaching and Facilitating.** As a leader, you must learn to stand up in front of people and get a point across, engaging others in the process. This doesn't come naturally to everyone. This chapter is full of tips and skill-building exercises that will make you a standout.

6. **Self-Awareness.** Know yourself. This is a key strength for leaders, but it takes time to reflect on your strengths, personality, fears, the way you think, and more. We can't be good at everything. First, we have to realize what we are and are not good at so that we can maximize our strengths and manage what may never be our strong suits. This chapter gives you many avenues for this exploration.

7. **Difficult Conversations and Coaching.** You may revisit this chapter more than once. Conflict and coaching conversations are never easy, nor should they be, but they can make a huge and positive impact when handled with skill. Look here for tips on sharing meaningful feedback, leading through the challenges of change, and effectively managing conflict.

8. **Diversity.** Diverse teams are strong teams when we appreciate people's differences and treat everyone with respect. This chapter highlights select diversities and provides lessons for recognizing biases, seeing people as unique individuals, and leading fairly and respectfully.

9. **Teamwork.** Teams are how we work. This chapter points out ways to make your teams work well together, no matter how they came together.

10. **Culture.** Culture rules, and leaders play a huge role in creating it. Culture can seem a little difficult to get your arms around. This chapter offers many ways that you can work toward creating a culture of retention and high morale.

11. **Push Yourself.** One of the few assumptions you can make is that there is always more to learn; never stop learning. We don't grow when we are comfortable. We grow when we are in that sweet spot of "I think I can. . . . I'm not 100 percent sure, but I believe I can do this." Go to this chapter for suggestions on broadening the scope of your leadership.

ORGANIZATION OF THE BOOK

Each chapter is broken down into sections that delve into specific topics. At the beginning of each chapter, you will find a brief self-assessment of the competencies covered in that chapter. Start here to determine which section will be most helpful for you. The scoring for each competency is as follows:

1—I am struggling with or not yet skilled at this.

2—I am starting to work on improving at this, but I need more skill building.

3—I am making some consistent progress in improving at this.

4—I am doing very well in this area.

No one needs to see this score but you—so be honest. Scoring a 1 or 2 indicates an area that likely needs your attention, and the self-assessment questions point you to sections that will be most helpful. A score of 3 indicates that you are doing well, and reading this section will support you in going from good to great. If you rate yourself a 4, your strength gives you the opportunity to mentor others, and reading this section can help you dissect just how you can do that and be a more effective mentor.

To assess yourself from a different angle, each section begins with a question prompting you to explore how growth in that area could benefit you and connecting you to the information that you need today.

In each section, you can expect to find the following:

- Coaching tips to take action immediately. It is like a "coach in a book."
- Reflection questions to make you think about and look at your situation from a fresh perspective.
- Ideas for sharing the content with your colleagues as part of a self-led leadership development session.
- Adaptable ideas for teaching, with content written in a way that spurs discussion and group work and can be expanded for assignments.

You will see some overlap among topics. Looking at a concept from different angles can aid learning.

What not to expect here: *The* one way to lead.

My intention in writing this book is that you sort that out for yourself. In my dad's eulogy, my siblings and I quoted him as often saying, "If I were you . . ." While we realized that he may have been right more often than we would have liked to admit, we still learned by doing things our own way. Evolving into your best leader-self is like that, too. I hope the ideas in this book spur your thinking, push you to consider and reflect on a deeper level, and decide for yourself how you want to be remembered as a leader.

Got five minutes? Let's get started!

CHAPTER 1

Communication

IF YOU HAVE had great role models in the area of communication, consider yourself lucky, because there is a serious communication skill gap everywhere you look. This chapter is the biggest in this book, and in truth, much of the content could fit here. The most common concern I hear from employee groups is "There is not enough communication around here!" You have probably heard it, too, or even said it yourself. As I have dug into what people are really asking for when they make this complaint, the topics in this chapter line up with what I think are the essential skills for leaders.

SELF-ASSESSMENT SCORING:

1—I am struggling with or not yet skilled at this.

2—I am starting to work on improving at this, but I need more skill building.

3—I am making some consistent progress in improving at this.

4—I am doing very well in this area.

Determine your current level of skill on these communication competencies (score 1–4):

1. I balance advocating my point of view with eliciting input from others through inquiry, and I can flex my communication approach to connect with the person I am speaking to. Score: _____

2. I use a variety of techniques to actively listen. Score: _____

3. My decisions to use electronic or face-to-face communication are clear and thoughtful. Score: _____

4. When I speak, I am aware of how my words impact my message, both positively and negatively. Score: _____

5. When people don't get on board right away with my well-thought-out plans, I use effective communication skills to focus on understanding their point of view rather than get frustrated with their resistance. Score: _____

6. I am aware of my use of "I'm sorry" and say it with meaning only when I am accepting appropriate personal accountability. Score: _____

7. Collaboration comes naturally to me, and I freely allow for shared ownership of projects, even when I know the benefits will go to others. Score: _____

8. I realistically navigate my expectations of myself and others. Score: _____

9. I am skilled at holding key conversations, such as getting a new employee off to the right start, setting the right tone in managing a former manager, or addressing gossip. Score: _____

10. I am confident and comfortable in my personal leadership power. Score: _____

11. I have a vision for my team/organization, and I can articulate that vision in such a way that others want to get on board with me. Score: _____

12. When it comes to translating a message between others (e.g., as a middle manager does between a senior team and frontline employees), I can effectively communicate both the message and my concerns. Score: _____

13. My messages are transparent and open even when doing so is not comfortable for me, and I can discern when transparency is appropriate and when it is not. Score: _____

Now explore the corresponding sections that follow to learn how to improve skills that need work or enhance your current skills.

1. ADVOCACY AND INQUIRY: BALANCING TWO APPROACHES TO COMMUNICATION

Do some people want you to be more direct? Or, conversely, do people bristle at your directness? This section will help most if someone is rubbing you the wrong way or feels that way about you when you communicate. Some people respond better to clear direction, while others prefer a more eliciting approach. Most of us lean in one direction or the other— either more advocacy or more inquiry. This section helps you assess which direction you lean and then modify and adapt your communication style to meet the needs of the person you want to influence.

You can improve your communication (and most of us want or need to) by first identifying your own communication wiring. One lens through which to consider your communication style is whether you use more *advocacy* or *inquiry* (Senge 1990). In a nutshell, advocacy (A) is communicating to state your position. Here are some examples of advocacy:

- I think it's important for you to try _____.
- Here is why this matters.
- This is what I need to see.
- I will do _____ for you.
- I believe _____ because _____.

Inquiry (I) is communicating in a manner that nudges others to reveal their thinking. Here are some examples of inquiry:

- Can you walk me through how you came to your decision?
- What's the best possible outcome you can imagine in this situation?
- How can you make this happen?
- How can I help?
- How do you see your role in this project?

We all use a mix of A and I, but most of us are more comfortable using one style than the other. If you aren't sure how you come across when you are communicating, ask for feedback from someone you work with regularly. Ask the person to read these examples and identify which way you are more likely to come across in your communication.

It's easy to see that each communication style has its strengths. Strong advocators are more likely to let you know where they stand, and they are more definitive, removing uncertainty. Those who are skilled in inquiry elicit more ideas than they could come up with alone, and they leave people feeling important for being asked.

Like any strength, though, either approach can create problems when you rely too heavily on it. Too much advocacy may make others feel as if their ideas don't matter or that it is not OK to disagree or discuss. Too much inquiry can feel like an interrogation or lead to endless options, never landing on a decision.

Clear communication is achieved through a *balance* of advocacy and inquiry—fancy words for *reveal your thinking* and *probe thoughtfully*, with a good dose of *listen well* added in.

Tips for the A's:

- After advocating your point, ask others to challenge your thinking and keep an open mind. The best results come from lively dialogue.
- If it feels like using inquiry is slowing things down, make inquiry a "task" on your to-do list. It is worth a few extra minutes to get the other person's best thinking.
- Consider: When do you have the opportunity to ask for input and show that you are willing to truly consider it?

Tips for the I's:

- Remember, stating your point clearly doesn't mean you are being "bossy."
- Advocating doesn't close the door to further dialogue. Others want to know what you think, too.
- Find opportunities to make a clear statement ending with a period.

2. LISTENING PRACTICE

Is stopping to really listen a challenge for you? The trouble with communication is that we worry more about what to say than how to listen. You'll notice that listening comes up in different ways throughout this book. Being a skilled listener puts you far ahead of most people in terms of leadership and relationships. This section focuses on daily practices to build your listening muscle—a crucial half of the communication equation.

Could you improve your listening skills? Most of us could. It is hard work—it's not called *active* listening for nothing. Practice one of these actions each day for the next five days and see what happens.

Day 1: Make a list. List the top ten people you interact with every week, whether at home or at work. Now, rate yourself on how well you listen to each one on a scale of 1 to 5 (where 1 indicates "I tune this person out most of the time" and 5 is "I am listening completely, understanding clearly, and can reflect this understanding back to this person"). Which scores are worth improving? Circle the names of the people with whom you will practice rigorous listening.

Day 2: Forget about remembering what you were going to say. This is one of the most common excuses for not listening well. We chomp at the bit to say what is on our mind before we forget. Will the world end if we do forget? Sometimes, it is more important to understand the other person than to spill your guts. If what you were planning to say is important, you will remember it later. Spend a day letting go of what you want to say while someone else is talking and focus on listening and understanding their message.

Day 3: Stop what you are doing. Turn toward the person who is speaking to you (this will help them feel important). Make eye contact, lay your hands in your lap, and open your ears. Spend a day turning directly toward the people who are speaking to you and do nothing else but listen—no typing, texting, reading, doodling, Googling, looking at a screen, or any other form of multi-tasking. Multi-tasking implies that we can successfully focus on several things at once, which is not true. My word for this is "multi-distracting," which means that none of our tasks are getting the attention they deserve.

Day 4: Close your mouth. No kidding! Can you wait until the other person is *completely* finished speaking their words—and *even a few extra seconds*—before you respond?

Doing so takes conscious effort. For one day, work at pausing for a few seconds after the other person finishes speaking. Becoming conscious of how often we interrupt others can be enlightening. It is amazing what we hear when we let people finish!

Day 5: Reflect first what you heard. In quality dialogue, both parties share their thoughts. Before you launch into what *you* think, respond to the other person's comments: "So you would like to . . . and it sounds like that would lead to . . . as you see it, is that right?" Then allow the other person to say "yes, that's correct," or "no that's not quite what I meant" and encourage them to clarify.

At first, these listening skills may feel like they are slowing down your communication, but they pay dividends: improved relationships, less conflict, and increased trust. These benefits are the opposite of a slowdown.

3. ELECTRONIC VERSUS FACE-TO-FACE COMMUNICATION

Are your electronic communications sometimes misunderstood? Do you avoid having face-to-face conversations because texting and emailing seem less threatening? Some messages need your presence to be delivered effectively. This section reviews which messages can be delivered by email or text and which ones need an in-person conversation.

As a manager, it may seem more efficient to text or email when you need to communicate with your employees, especially if you manage virtually across multiple locations. You can't always communicate face-to-face, but how do you decide which type of communication is best? Consider these factors before hitting send:

Email usually works for these kinds of communications:

- Reviewing or clarifying the steps in a process or a decision you have already discussed.
- Exchanging information that is not emotional for you or your employees.
- Reporting progress on a task or project that you or your employees have done before (it is not new or different).
- Communicating information when clear roles of responsibility are lacking.
- Touching base on a relationship that already has a sound basis of trust.
- Conveying the facts about issues that are not complex.
- Giving employees a heads-up about what you want to discuss in a meeting, especially if this is your regular way of doing business (e.g., "Every Monday, email me your agenda items for our coaching session, and I will add mine and return to you by Tuesday, so that we both know what we need to be prepared for").
- Offering praise and recognition.
- Following up on a face-to-face discussion to document the decisions or agreements made (e.g., "Here is my understanding of the agreement we came to in our discussion yesterday."

Face-to-face communications work best when:

- Emotions may be running high, or have the potential to.
- It is a coaching discussion about any kind of underperformance.
- You are conducting performance evaluations or goal-setting sessions.
- You need the person's buy-in.

- You need to establish a relationship of trust because the person is new or conflict has occurred in the past.
- The employee may not understand their role or boundaries.
- Collaboration is important to getting the job done.
- You are announcing a major change in the department.
- The discussion becomes a back-and-forth email conversation.
- The work is new territory, not something that has been done before.
- You want to recognize an employee who goes above and beyond the call of duty.
- The information will be hard to hear, particularly if it has not already been discussed.
- You are feeling out of touch with your employees.
- You hear concerns about employees from others but you have not seen the behaviors of concern yourself.

You can strengthen your leadership with these *intentional* communication practices:

- If you are emotional when you compose the email, walk away from it before you hit send. You are likely to regret it otherwise.
- For that matter, if you are emotional before a face-to-face conference, take some time to reflect and prepare ahead of time.
- If you are in doubt about sending an email or any kind of electronic communication, have a face-to-face conversation instead.
- Consider how people would rate your "presence" in the department. For some people, that means being accessible for in-person conversations once in a while.

- When you do use email, simple things can matter more than you might think and help you engage with people.
  - Use a greeting and personal names.
  - Thank people.
  - Know that CAPITALIZED LETTERS are often misinterpreted as anger.
  - Include a signature with your contact information on all messages you send so that people can get in touch with you easily.
- Texting, while informal, is ubiquitous. But it is also ripe for misunderstanding, because of its brevity, shorthand, and symbols and emojis. Ask yourself—how might this text message be misunderstood?

4. WORDS ARE POWERFUL

Are you are using language that shuts down communication before it even starts? Some words set you up to be misunderstood. The list of terms in this section is not exhaustive, but it can help you think about the ways you express yourself and avoid unintentionally getting in your own way.

Most people agree that actions speak louder than words—but that does not mean words don't have an influence. Some of the words we use may interfere with our ability to earn respect or be seen as an effective leader. The idea is to think intentionally about how we speak and whether our words work *for* or *against* our employees' needs to feel respected, dignified, important, valuable, and successful. Here are a few words to consider:

Subordinate. Managers often use the word "subordinate" to refer to the people who report to them. This word might also be interpreted to mean less important, subservient, inferior, or lower—not words that most employees would consider motivating or inspiring. What is a better way to refer to the people whose best efforts and high engagement make *you* successful? Consider: "My team," "direct reports," "frontline employees."

LDI, HRSA, HIT, etc. Listen to your speech for acronyms and initialisms. We use them so often as handy shortcuts, but we assume that everyone knows what we are talking about. Employees may feel foolish if they have to ask, and when questions go unasked, we don't speed up at all. It is better to assume that everyone does not know what an acronym stands for. Consider: Say it the way you write it, with the acronym followed by the spelled-out version, at least the first time.

"Leader" versus "manager." Many of us use these terms interchangeably. I was once challenged on this one. I tended to call all people in official positions of management "leaders" without differentiating between the two terms. An employee who was not a manager asked me if I thought nonmanagers could be leaders in their role, and of course I said yes. He then asked why I kept referring to "leadership" as if it were synonymous with "management." The words I was using made him feel that he couldn't be a leader if he was not a manager. Point taken. Consider: Name the person you are referring to. If not everyone is a manager, then say "leaders."

I'm a perfectionist. When you tell your employees that you are a perfectionist, what they hear is that you expect them to be perfect, too. We want employees to openly discuss their mistakes so that we can all learn from them and to be willing to ask questions when they are unsure. Expectations of perfection shut the door on those kinds of conversations. Consider: Strive for excellence instead of perfection.

I/Me. It's easy to slip into using I/me when we are so invested in our work. Consider: Watch for opportunities to say us/we when you can. It's more inclusive, and it keeps your ego in check.

The girls. Referring to a department made up of all women as "the girls" will be offensive to most grown women. When I heard this term used, I don't believe the manager *intended* it to be belittling—but if I had been one of those "girls," it would have felt that way. It doesn't come across as empowering, and there are better options. Consider: "The team."

You guys. We all say "you guys" without giving it a thought. But *guys* are only about half the population. Like "the girls," it may be hard to see why this matters if you are not the one feeling left out or having to adapt to a description that doesn't include you. Consider: "Everyone," "folks," or "y'all" are better terms to get a group's attention without leaving anyone out.

Blah, blah, blah. You know it when you hear it. You try to follow the speaker, but your mind drifts off, and you start thinking about what you need to pick up from the grocery store. Intelligent words come out of a speaker's mouth, but all you hear is "blah, blah, blah." When we use buzzwords and jargon, we lose people. Consider: Watch your language to make sure you are not overdoing it, and watch your listener for signs of that glazed look that tells you they may not be listening to you.

5. DO YOU WANT TO BE RIGHT . . . OR EFFECTIVE?

Have you ever felt that you were right, but instead of agreement, you met with resistance? This section helps you move past frustration to a place of influence.

Have you ever heard of Dr. Ignaz Semmelweis? He was the man known—long after his death in 1865—as the father of infection control. Semmelweis discovered the connection between hand-washing and infection prevention, but he was unsuccessful at convincing people to change their habits. Sometimes being right is easier than being *effective*.

Semmelweis's ineffective approach prevented him from being recognized for his discovery during his lifetime, well before others more influential came to the same conclusion. An article in the *British Medical Journal* (McArdle, Ali, and Brown 2007) tells the story of his mistakes and explains why he was ineffective at getting people to accept a new and better way of doing things.

Here are some things that Semmelweis did that were not helpful:

- Didn't share important data
- Published his findings but wrote so poorly that no one could understand him
- Tried to humiliate people into changing their habits
- Acted arrogantly and righteously (he was right, after all!)
- Insulted people who disagreed with him
- Accused senior leaders of harmful intent when they clung to their beliefs
- Divided people by creating an "us against them" mentality
- Abandoned his supporters when he didn't get his way

While we can't underestimate the culture's desire for the status quo (after all, we don't have 100 percent compliance with hand-washing even today), many lessons can be learned from Semmelweis's experience. What could Semmelweis have done differently, and how can we apply those lessons to changes we are trying to make today?

Data talks, %^(*#* walks. If you are right, data will back you up. How can you document what you are attempting to do with data?

Make your data understandable. Complicated charts and graphs that don't connect the dots for people will be ignored. What will make the change interesting *from the audience's perspective*? Tell that story.

Start with mutual respect. Shaming people into change is a strategy for failure. As in conflict resolution, when you have two opposing views, consider the points on which you agree. What do you and those resisting the change both want? How can you make it safe to have a dialogue?

Display genuine humility. Arrogance may work if you don't need people, but the opposite—humility—makes you more approachable when you can't do it alone. When we know we are right, it can be so satisfying that we don't see our own arrogance. Find a peer you trust to tell you the truth. Ask, "How do I come across when I talk about my idea? Do I leave room for others to share the credit? Do I step on anyone's toes? Am I understandable? How am I managing my defensiveness when others disagree?"

Invite and welcome questions rather than insult those who disagree with you. Don't perceive questions as personal attacks. This is an opportunity to engage skeptics and reach understanding. Manage your defensiveness by reminding yourself that questions—by forcing you to clarify your arguments—can help you improve your idea and ultimately gain support.

Assume good intent. Most senior leaders don't lie awake at night strategizing how they can block your good ideas. If they can't see it, demonstrate how your idea will help them succeed. Are you frustrated because you didn't get the answer you wanted? Consider, even ask, what leaders need to be convinced to give you a try? What details, big picture plans, system issues, people or other resources, barriers, etc., might be on their radar that you have overlooked? Then address those.

Change begs for win-win. To succeed at implementing change, you need to engage a majority of people to get behind you. You can't do it alone. Think of the power that Semmelweis's small group of supportive colleagues could have wielded in infection control if they had focused on reaching out and positively influencing the masses, communicating effectively, and shaking hands (washed, of course) with those whose support they sought. Who do you need to reach out to? It may be the person or group you least want to engage, but whose support could help you the most.

Take the long view. It is tempting to give up in the face of resistance, but your supporters need you to persevere. Much innovation, particularly in healthcare, takes *years* to go from research to practice. It rarely goes as quickly as we would like (often because of the same mistakes that Semmelweis made).

6. SAYING "I'M SORRY"

How and when do you apologize? Do you wonder whether your apologies are taken seriously? In this section, explore the right time and place for saying you are sorry—and when not to.

The way most of us use the phrase "I'm sorry" is a bit like the childhood story of Goldilocks and the Three Bears: too much, too little, or just right. It is worth the effort to get apologies right. People perceive a lot about our self-confidence and integrity when we do—or do not—apologize and mean it.

Too much. I knew a manager who actually said "I'm sorry" instead of "Hello" when she entered a room. While she brought wonderful creativity to plans, she was nearly always late, disorganized, and disheveled. People began to *expect* her to say she was sorry . . . and to be late, disorganized, and disheveled. Her apology came to have no meaning whatsoever, and it was so unfortunate for this talented woman that "sorry" became a word that people used to describe her. Even if "I'm sorry" is not your greeting, do you tend to over-apologize?

"I'm sorry, but I am going to have to ask you to be at work on time." Do we really regret that we have a policy of being on time for work? Are we at fault for someone else's lack of self-management? If not, then it is dishonest to say that *you* are sorry.

"I'm so sorry, but I am going to have to put this disciplinary note in your personnel file." Did you commit the infraction? If not, then you don't have anything to apologize for.

Here is the mix-up: We feel uncomfortable, believing that we are causing the other person to feel bad by giving voice to the way they have missed the mark. When we examine what led to the discussion, we did not cause it. We apologize to soften the blow, but does it? More often, the apology creates the perception that we are unsure of ourselves, and it doesn't take away any discomfort for the person who is being held accountable. In fact, some discomfort is helpful in motivating behavior change. Do you say "I'm sorry" to manage your own discomfort? Practice delivering a tough message assertively and without apology. Use a mirror, write it out, or rehearse with your manager.

Too little. Most of us also know individuals who never utter the words "I'm sorry," even when doing so would begin to repair what is broken. Old school management advises, "Never let them see you sweat, or make a mistake, or be unsure of yourself." But who is that person who never sweats, who is always correct, who is always certain? No one.

In politics, apologizing is often seen as a sign of weakness. For example, in 2012, the deputy prime minister of the United Kingdom faced ridicule for apologizing for the government's broken promises on tuition fees (Grice 2012). So strong is the political rule against apologies that he responded, "What, you want me to apologize for apologizing?"

If we never show that *we* make mistakes, then it is disingenuous to say "let's learn from our mistakes." Employees see that perfection is the expectation, and that kind of pressure leads to an environment of increased errors because people are fearful of speaking up. Do you hesitate to say you are sorry in front of your team? How could you improve the openness of your department culture if you used one of your "mistakes" to create dialogue about improvement?

Just right. "I'm sorry. I thought this new process was going to work, but it looks like there are some things that I didn't think about before putting it into action." This is a genuine apology: You made a decision that did not turn out well, and it shows honesty that you can tell people that you are human too. It says that mistakes can be learning opportunities for everyone.

"I'm sorry that I was not clearer in my directive." Be careful with this one. If you made assumptions in your communication with someone that led to a misunderstanding, then it is fair to take ownership of that. Then take steps to improve your message clarity the next time. Try asking after giving an assignment, "Tell me how you understand what I am looking for in this project." Don't let "I'm sorry" become a backup plan for not following through or communicating clearly.

Today, examine your reasons when you do—or choose not to—say "I'm sorry."

7. CAN WE COLLABORATE?

> **Do you find it hard to give up control in some situations? Does your sense of ownership prevent you from allowing others an equal place at the table?** You are not alone. Collaboration is harder than it sounds, but the benefits are greater when we get it right. This section offers reflection and communication tips for improving your ability to lead collaboratively.

Cooperation is great, but the word is not interchangeable with *collaboration*. Consider that in a true collaboration, *all parties must give up something to achieve the greater good*. Cooperation is like parallel play among toddlers (independently and peacefully playing side by side with different toys) versus the preschool phase of learning about sharing. We realize—as hard as it may be—that if you share your coloring book with me, and I share my crayons with you, everybody wins. I guess we actually needed to begin learning about collaboration *before* kindergarten!

Collaboration sounds easy and obvious, and it can be sometimes. But when opinions clash, resources are scarce, or priorities differ, collaboration is an effort that requires technical and interpersonal skills. But it is worthwhile. It can get you more than you could ever achieve alone.

You have control over only one voice—your own. Here are some things you can do to build your skills in leading collaboration:

- **Decide why collaboration is in your best interest.** Is there something big you want to achieve? Could it be more attainable with the support of others? When you ask for support, make sure to find out what is in it for others, too.

- **Identify together a clear purpose that is in everyone's interest.** This is your guiding light in times of personal agendas and flaring egos. Direct the group toward the clear mutual purpose when competition threatens to overtake collaboration.

- **Look for opportunities to share the credit.** In a management position, you may get praise for the accomplishments of the collaboration. To keep the collaboration alive, take those moments to point out the contributions of the group members. This is one of those times when it doesn't cost much to be a good person.

- **Balance "process" and "outcome."** The dilemma: You won't reach your deliverables if you don't maintain relationships, and you won't maintain relationships if you don't eventually deliver. You have to do both. If your personality is more attuned to the agenda, partner with someone who has a strong intuitive sense of how the people process is working, and vice versa.

- **More collaboration means less control.** Can you get more comfortable with that? What are you giving up if you let go of some of the control?

- **Create a "go-to" mantra** for when the going gets messy. For example, "It may take longer to work together, but it will last longer if we do."

- **Empathy goes a long way.** Conflicts pop up when we see things differently. The old adage "seek first to understand" softens communication, opens doors to understanding, and allows you to build from there. You can't build from a stalemate, so start by empathizing. When you feel at odds with a team member, practice asking yourself, "How would I see this situation if I were in her shoes?" or, "What would help him feel heard and understood?" Listen and understand: It doesn't mean you have to agree.

- **Eliminate jargon.** It's safe to assume that if you use a lot of jargon, some people will feel left out. Many of them will never tell you about it because they don't want to look foolish. When you lose them, you lose your influence, so strive to keep your communication as clear as possible.

- **Good facilitation skills take the "personal" out of differences.** They help people process their thinking, make decisions that benefit the larger purpose, and keep the focus on team.

If you are not skilled in facilitation tools, either add someone to the team who has these skills or learn them yourself. Try this one: End your meeting with a "fist to five" evaluation (Schoenholz and Burkhart-Kriesel 2008). Ask everyone, at the same time, to indicate by a show of hands their level of commitment to the group's decisions today. A fist (zero) indicates no commitment at all; five fingers signals complete commitment. For anything less than a five, ask what it would take to get to a five from everyone, or even for people to move up just one number.

8. MANAGING YOUR EXPECTATIONS

Have you been disappointed in others when they should have known what you expected? Do you feel like you expect too much or too little of yourself or others? This section provides reflections for being more conscious and deliberate about your expectations.

More than a classic Charles Dickens title, "great expectations" are a part of everyday life. Consciously or unconsciously, most of us ask ourselves these questions every day:

- What do I expect of myself today?
- What do I expect of others?
- What difference or impact will it make if I do—or don't— meet my own or others' expectations of me?

- How will I communicate my expectations?
- Are my expectations fair?

Consider these reflections on "great expectations":

Optimistic expectations alone won't cut it. Remember the Affordable Care Act website debacle that threw everyone into a tailspin when it locked up in the early days of implementation? (Harvard Business School 2016). What if the message to the public before the launch had been that the website would likely act like any new website and that delays and problems were *expected*. A statement such as "Here is what we can expect in a worst-case scenario, and this is how we will address it if that happens" could have been helpful in preventing some frustration. Optimists may have the edge when it comes to longevity and physical and mental health, but when optimism blocks awareness of realistic downsides, plans can backfire. Believe in people *and* preempt uproar by acknowledging what could go wrong and sharing your plan for addressing glitches if expectations are not met.

Don't expect anything and you won't be disappointed. How sad. This phrase makes me want to pull the covers over my head and not even try. Obviously born from previous disappointments, this statement is not very motivating. But the lesson is that even if it is hard to do so, we have to "manage" our expectations, just as we have to manage our anger in a conflict or manage our fear when speaking in public. Try this reframing: "I'll expect the best from myself and know that whatever the outcome, I will have met my own expectations."

For those to whom much is given, much is expected. Unlike the last statement, this message gets me out of bed. It's the heart of the idea of servant leadership, articulated by Robert Greenleaf. The foundation of servant leadership is that leaders expect that they will serve others rather than expect others to serve them. Ask yourself: What are my gifts and talents? Who could benefit from them? How can I share them to meet others' needs? What am I grateful for? How can I push myself to "pay it forward"?

They should have known what I expected! Maybe they should have, but they didn't. Perhaps I neglected to explain what I expected. Perhaps I assumed that they were in sync with what was in my head (it was so clear to me, after all!). Perhaps I did *tell* them, and I assumed that they *understood*—two very different things. If you are disappointed in people because they ought to have known, you may need to be clearer in expressing your expectations. If your inner thought is "I shouldn't *have* to tell them," that is a good indication that you probably need to. This is especially true if you hope that your own example is enough to demonstrate what is expected of others. You can never stop being a role model, but you can't rely on that to be enough. Examine your expectations of others—even what seems obvious to you—by making a list. Share that list as a starting point for a dialogue in which the intention is to understand *mutual* expectations.

Suspend your expectation biases. A common bias in the workplace is older workers believing younger professionals should act like they did when they entered the workforce. However, one of the qualities of managers who are successful with millennials is the ability to set aside what you *expect* them to be (like you at their age) and to consider where they actually *are* in their development (which, because of different parenting and societal norms, can mean they are at a different—not better or worse—maturational place upon entering the workforce). Tip: Develop the patience to meet people where they are instead of where you think they should be. The relationship you establish will be the foundation for setting—and meeting—expectations going forward.

One thing is clear: Everyone has a different opinion about whether expectations should even be acknowledged. It is natural to wrestle with them: How can you make expectations work for you?

9. THREE PIVOTAL CONVERSATIONS: NEW EMPLOYEE, MANAGING A FORMER MANAGER, AND INVITATION TO GOSSIP

> **Do you have a new employee you want to start off on the right foot? Are you managing a former manager? Has someone tempted you to gossip?** These three conversations, which most leaders will face at some point, can benefit from thoughtful communication. This section provides some simple tips.

When it comes to communicating at turning points, I am a fan of stating the obvious. When something seems obvious, we often do not voice our thinking. This can be a missed opportunity to make things better or prevent misunderstandings. Here are three communication junctures where leaders can make a big difference in the long run, along with suggestions for having the conversation:

When you have a new employee. Bringing a new employee on board requires many important conversations. I learned about one conversation decades ago from an accomplished colleague, Cella Janisch-Hartline, a nurse consultant. She teaches preceptors—those who are mentoring and onboarding new hires—about "setting the stage." Here is how that conversation might sound:

- "I want you to be successful here! That is my intention when I give feedback on your performance. I will tell you when I see you hitting the mark, and I will also give you feedback when I see something that is getting in the way of your success—whether it is a technical skill or a behavior that may undermine you." Setting the stage allows both of you to have difficult conversations in the future, because you can always reference back to the purpose of your feedback—the employee's success. It may be less painful for the employee to hear and less likely that you will avoid giving the feedback.

- "You bring a fresh set of eyes. Talk to us about your experience, especially during these first few months. Help us be better, too." Maybe you already say this, but do you mean it? Too often, we either forget to check in and ask genuinely, or we get defensive if the employee says anything that is less than positive. Even if we're not openly guarded, we have to make it easier for employees to tell us what they see—something that is uncomfortable for most new employees to do. Decide to mean it when you say it, and respond to any negative comments by saying "Tell me more about that," rather than getting defensive.

- "A year from now, what would you like to be able to say about your first year?" This will tell you volumes about what a new employee is going to need from you. Investing in a retention plan unique to each employee makes it more likely that new hires will stay.

- Follow up on the previous question: "How would I know if you were struggling in this first year?" Don't accept "Oh, you'll know" for an answer. Many new employees, especially those with experience in other organizations or roles, underestimate their learning curve. Ask them to think about what struggling might look like for them, what they may or may not say about it, and what would help them feel more comfortable in speaking up and asking you for help.

When you are managing a former manager. This is a tricky situation, especially if the person was *your* former manager. You both need the transition to go well, but there are pitfalls, even when it is a voluntary role change for the former manager. Role changes require a shift in perception on everyone's part and can leave people with a lack of clarity. Sometimes differences in age or experience add to the challenge of employees fully placing you in the manager role. Most former managers don't intend to undermine you, but may do so unknowingly. To prevent problems, you might try the following starters with the former manager:

- "I'd really like your support." This is stating the obvious, but you can't assume support—so be bold and ask for it directly.
- "Here's what your support would look like: (fill in the blank)." *Do* fill in the blank. The word "support" means different things to different people so be specific. Have a dialogue:
  - "When employees come to you with supervisory issues, let's discuss how you can respond." Making this a dialogue instead of telling the person exactly what you want them to say engages you both in the solution and gets their buy-in.
  - Once you settle the first issue, follow up: "Now let's talk about other issues that might come up because of the role change so that we are both ready for them." Shed light on any potential problems before they occur, prepare—even role play—for them, and reconnect around your shared goal of the team's success.

When someone wants to engage you in gossip. Most workplaces offer plenty of opportunities for us to practice this pivotal conversation. The response is simple: "I'm not comfortable talking about this person when they aren't here." If you have gossiped in the past (most of us have), you might say, "I know I have talked about this person with you before, but I don't feel good about it. I need to stop. If one of us has a concern with her, we need to talk with her directly." Wouldn't it be amazing if we all committed to this?

10. STEPPING INTO YOUR OWN POWER

> **Do you ever feel uncomfortable with the power of your leadership role? Are you aware of the power that you do—or do not—communicate?** This exploration of what power means to you as a leader can help you grow into using your power for the greater good.

People are weird about power, and often they are uncomfortable with it. Some leaders will say things like, "I don't think I am that powerful." This attempt at humility may be well intended, but you are probably wrong. Power is a quality that leaders don't self-assess very accurately. You likely have more power than you think you do, and you may not be taking full advantage of it to make the right things happen.

When a judge pounds the gavel, it is a powerful and effective request for order. The ability to punish others, along with the judge's formal position of authority, are examples of two of the five power sources described by social psychologists French and Raven (1959) in their research on power—and they are the two sources of power that make most people uncomfortable. The other three sources of power in this model are also fruitful ones to cultivate for employee engagement. Build power that comes from:

- The respect others have for you (earned by your actions of integrity over time)
- The ability to reward others (even if you can't give people a raise, there are many ways to reward and recognize)

- Your expertise (through these three words: "In my experience . . .")

Unexamined power has consequences. We miss seeing how our behavior undermines others' efforts and can hurt relationships, but we also miss opportunities to support growth and change. The higher your position, the more you are noticed. Like it or not, your presence has power. Explore using your power intentionally.

Are you too self-conscious to claim it? I have noticed leadership workshop participants folding their program evaluations so that others can't see what they have written. Many people are self-conscious, wanting to avoid being judged as lacking in some way. As you grow in your leadership, remember that awareness of your power is connected to self-confidence: What are you confident about? Do you see others following your lead even if you haven't directly asked them to? Would you be surprised to hear others say that you have power? What opportunities can you take to speak up, step up to a new task, or advocate for someone or something? What could you start, do, or achieve if you *believed* in your power—if you could just let go of your self-consciousness?

The wisdom to know the difference. We reduce our own suffering when we discern what we have power over and what we don't. We may influence others through coaching or nudging them, but ultimately we don't have power over their actions. What is within your power when it comes to other people's behavior and decisions? What do you need to give yourself permission to act on or decide? Conversely, what are you forcing?

"Hello, power, I'd like you to meet my ego." Some people resist claiming the power that is rightfully theirs for fear of abusing their power. In other cases, ego may be operating without explicit permission. Positional power (we are the boss) becomes destructive when we lose perspective, when we do things just because we can. Who keeps you in check? What relationships ground you, and who will tell you when you have gone too far? Cultivate a relationship like this for your own balance.

Power doesn't have to be loud and "out front." Think of people you respect who are able to make things happen. Many different styles of power can be effective. The secret is to make the best use of your natural preferences and style. What are your personality strengths? Ask a trusted colleague, "How do you think I could more effectively make use of my strengths? What do I do or say that minimizes my power?"

11. COMMUNICATING A VISION

Do you know your destination but have a hard time keeping everyone on the same path? Setting a clear vision takes effort but is worthwhile. This section offers some tips for creating a vision that will inspire others.

Gundersen Health System in western Wisconsin went "off the grid" in 2014—the first hospital in the nation to do so by decreasing consumption and manufacturing its own energy through wind power and landfill gas-to-energy initiatives. Doing so was a big deal, considering the amount of energy it takes to run a hospital. With this move, the hospital began to produce more energy than it consumed. When CEO Jeff Thompson stated in the Gundersen Health System newsletter in 2015, "We set out to make the air better for our patients to breathe," I thought, now *that* is a vision statement I'll bet people can remember! A vision is meant to inspire, and this one nails it.

Perfect, complex, grammatically correct phrases might look beautiful, but they may not chart the course as you hope. We have good intentions: We want to look smart, want to have our vision reflect well on our organization, and we want others to know that we spent a lot of time thinking it through. But do your words achieve your goal, which is to ignite the enthusiasm of others so that they buy into your vision?

If it's not memorable, it's not worth it. Groups of smart, well-intentioned leaders often fumble when asked to recall the exact wording of their organization's vision statement. They get embarrassed because they can't recite it exactly. But if the words do not connect with their heart and soul, it is really just memorization. When the vision is vague, you will get somewhere, but it may not be where you intended.

Ask employees to rewrite your vision statement in their own words. Ask, "If we do our best work today, what is possible for our customers five to ten years from now?" Keep it to one sentence. You might end up replacing the plaque on the wall.

Speak to people's emotions. Consider the difference between these two statements: "We are going to make the air better for our patients to breathe" versus "We are going to control our electricity costs." Gundersen achieved both goals, but the former vision statement inspired more people to get behind it.

Simplify. Can you say it in one sentence? Write a paragraph if you must, but craft one brief statement that summarizes your vision in words that people can wrap their arms around.

Make it bold. Consider the vision statement of the Rural Wisconsin Health Cooperative: "Rural Wisconsin communities will be the healthiest in the nation" (RWHC 2020). It's audacious, clear, and *hopeful*. Every day in our work, we can ask ourselves, "Is what I am doing today making this vision happen?"

Take people someplace they want to go. In their book *Switch: How to Change Things When Change Is Hard* (2010), Chip and Dan Heath describe a "destination postcard." Using words, paint a picture of where you are headed, and people will want to go there with you.

The most powerful vision statements are ten words or fewer, since the words they use pack a punch. Consider, for example, the vision of Habitat for Humanity International (2020): "A world where everyone has a decent place to live." Clear. To the point. Everything the organization does is lined up with making that vision a reality.

In healthcare, to keep the doors open, we must have high-quality, cost-effective, and accessible care. Writing a vision goes beyond that. What makes *you* stand out? What is unique about what *you* can achieve?

12. CASCADING A MESSAGE—ESPECIALLY WHEN YOU MIGHT NOT AGREE WITH IT

Have you ever felt stuck trying to pass a message between senior leaders and those who report to you because the message is unclear, unpopular, or otherwise unpleasant? Middle managers often must act as translators, and more than words are at stake. In this section, learn some key points for communicating your needs and seeing the long-term impact of how you handle these challenging situations.

"Cascading" conjures up a waterfall flowing from a mystical source downward into a large body of water, something lovely and mesmerizing to see. It is not always so when "cascading" is used as a term for spreading an organizational message to all employees. Though the intent is to communicate a clear message, too frequently, something is lost in translation. In the leader's head it sounds like, "This is going to be great!" When transmitted, the message is heard like this:

- "What the heck were they talking about? I wonder if I'm the only one who doesn't understand."
- "This initiative is going to go away and something different will replace it next week, so why bother getting everyone all upset? I'll just wait and see."
- "I don't know how I'm going to get this done with everything else I have going on. It goes on my back burner."
- "This is never going to work on the front lines. My staff is going to go crazy when they hear this. I will tell them we have to do it, but that I am totally against it and on their side."

A middle manager can feel pulled between senior leaders, who need you to communicate and take action, and the team, who counts on you to look out for them. As a translator, how can you cascade a message effectively if you don't understand it, agree with it, or like it?

Seek to understand. Ask questions of your leaders in a way that prevents defensiveness:

- "Can you help me understand this better—what it is, why we're doing this, how we will do it, who will be involved?" Make sure that you walk away with the what, why, how, and who, so that your translation will meet the needs of your audience.
- "How would you explain this to employees who might not like the idea?" Be ready for the resistance by thinking about it in advance.

- "What is the rationale behind this decision?" Get to the true rationale so that you can communicate to your audience what's in it for them.
- "What are our first steps and recognizable milestones so that we can measure our progress?" People are easily overwhelmed when a goal seems too big. Milestones provide motivation, reinforcement, perspective, and hope.
- "How will we know when we are successful?" This is a great question! It paints a picture of what it will look like when you have reached your goal, so that people have a clear target.
- "What three key points can I make in getting this message across to employees?" You may have to convey the message in a brief huddle—ask for help to get to the meat of the message.

Disagree respectfully if you must. Start by assuming good intent, that the initiative or directive is being given for a valid reason and a desire for success. Ask, "May I point out some concerns about how this may impact my department?" Stick to facts and observations and avoid drama and judgment. If you are reacting emotionally, manage yourself. Emotions are human and normal, but you don't want them to get in the way of your message. Breathe deeply! Also consider your timing, with respect to your own state of mind, the setting, and the current situation for the leader with whom you disagree.

Practice active listening. "Here is what I understood from what you said (summarizing the message)—do I have it right?" Doing this lets others know that you are listening before sharing your concerns. Leaders are more likely to listen to you when it's your turn. Ask your employees to practice this same technique when you meet with them.

Ask for help. "I want to have credibility in cascading this message when it is hard for me to accept it myself. Can you help me do this?" This builds trust between you and your leader that you are accepting accountability even when it is hard.

Don't throw anyone under the bus. Blaming others shows a lack of leadership. Don't let your words, body language, or actions communicate that if you were in charge, this unpopular change or initiative would not be happening. Remember that you are always part of leadership, and it is about maintaining your own—and your organization's— integrity. It might sound like this: "I hear your concerns, and I have brought them to senior leadership. In the end, this is a decision that is being made for the good of the organization. While not everyone is happy about it, I am committed to supporting it, and I need your commitment, too."

13. TRANSPARENCY

> **Does it seem like there is more to the story than what you are hearing? Is trust a concern, with people often speculating on hidden agendas or waiting for the other shoe to drop?** Learn what transparency really means, how to achieve it, and what to be transparent about in this section.

Back in the 1980s when I taught, I used transparencies, which were clear pieces of film written on with a marker, projected onto the wall from a lighted screen. Today, transparency means shining a light onto the truth.

The truth can be uncomfortable. An unwritten rule is deeply entrenched in our leadership culture that we must look good, smart, and right. This rule leads us to skirt the truth, which destroys our leadership credibility.

Transparency is a buzzword. I hear employees saying (and gurus recommending), "Leaders need to be more transparent." I watch leaders' frozen faces as they question, "Surely I am transparent, right?" Let's reflect on what transparency is and is not.

What transparency *is*:

- **Keeping people informed.** Inform in a way that connects to what is important to *them*, in language that makes sense to *them*, minus the jargon and the assumption that everyone knows what you know. They don't. Information vacuums are quickly filled with suspicion and drama that you will spend hours navigating.

- **Being vulnerable.** Don't dismiss vulnerability by thinking it means you have to open up about your personal life, cry, say "I love you," or any other mushy stuff. Vulnerability *does* mean:

  - Being honest, not sugar-coating or putting a spin on something. People can smell "spin" from a mile away.

  - Admitting you don't have all the answers, and never making them up. This makes you human, not flawed.

  - Owning up when you make a mistake. It is healing for everyone when a leader who has erred owns it.

  - Following up on that ownership with sincere change. "I'm sorry" is hollow if it is not followed by corrective action.

- **Exposing your data.** Put your quality data and strategic metrics up on the wall for all to see. No secrets. "This is where we are, where we are headed, and what we need to do to get where we want to go."

- **Unearthing your real agenda.** If you need support, say so. Be clear about what that support looks and sounds like. If you need something unpopular, it's alright to acknowledge that, but don't throw blame elsewhere.

- **Trusting your team.** Don't underestimate what people can handle. Most people can handle the truth much better than the worrying that accompanies silence and waiting for the other shoe to drop.

- **Matching actions and words.** "Walking the talk" is transparency at its best. Review your organization's excellence standards. Does your behavior match those standards? You can't hold others to those standards if you don't demonstrate them yourself. (If you don't have standards written out explicitly, take the opportunity to ask your team what excellence in service to each other looks like in terms of specific behaviors.)
- **Empowering.** One barrier to openness is the belief that you will lose power. This is a myth. Your superpower is your team, and teams are engaged when they understand your challenges. They can bring their great ideas and solutions to the table with a vested interest in the outcome.

What transparency *is not*:

- **Sharing confidential personnel information.** I once had to terminate an employee—someone who was beloved by colleagues, who did not see it coming. They wanted to know why their coworker was fired. I worked to build trust by letting them know that all personnel discussions are confidential, and they could count on me to honor private conversations. I also listened for what was not being said. The real concern was, "What gets a person fired here, and am I at risk?" Those are questions I could answer.
- **Telling all of your personal details.** People do want to know you as a person, but you get to decide what to share about your life outside of work. Try the "share-check-share" method. Open up a little and see how that goes, and take it from there.
- **Emailing.** Face-to-face conversations are required if you want people to know where you stand and find you

approachable. Electronic communication has its place, but you can't hide behind it and still be transparent.

- **A one-way street.** As you make space for others to be transparent, you may hear things that are not so easy to accept. When someone gives you honest feedback or disagrees with you, take care to manage your defensiveness.

Think of leaders you respect and admire. How do they demonstrate transparency?

CHAPTER 2

Inspiration

WE'RE EITHER GROWING or we're dying. Sometimes it takes a little inspiration to get excited about growth and learning—it doesn't always come to you. This chapter includes reflections and thought-provoking reminders of what matters most in the long run. You'll learn ways to move from where you are to where you dream of being.

SELF-ASSESSMENT SCORING:

1—I am struggling with or not yet skilled at this.

2—I am starting to work on improving at this, but I need more skill building.

3—I am making some consistent progress in improving at this.

4—I am doing very well in this area.

Determine your current level of skill on these inspiration competencies (score 1–4):

1.   Humility and wisdom are hardwired into my leadership.
     Score: _____

2. I know what is special about my leadership style, and I understand my strengths. Score: _____

3. I have a clear vision of my best self as a leader and a plan to get there. Score: _____

4. I bring my best talents and passion to my leadership every day. Score: _____

5. I demonstrate leadership behaviors daily by weaving them into real-time moments, not just plans for the future. Score: _____

6. I can get myself through a tough day with clear thinking and skills for correcting my perspective when things don't go as planned. Score: _____

7. I spend time listening to and observing successful leaders to learn from their experience and apply it to my own growth. Score: _____

Now explore the corresponding sections that follow to learn how to improve skills that need work or enhance your current skills.

1. GAINING WISDOM

Who do you think of as "wise"? Do you wonder how you can build wisdom into your leadership? The reflections in this section help you pursue wisdom intentionally.

Older . . . wiser?

These two words are not always connected by "and." Not only are some young people incredibly wise, there are definitely some older people who do not become wiser with age. Smart is one thing, but wise goes further. Do you aspire to be a wise leader?

I think of Nelson Mandela. The Dalai Lama. Eleanor Roosevelt. My mom and dad. This is a diverse list with some common threads, but one quality in particular stands out: They were all forgiving, even when it was not easy to do so. Who comes to mind when you think of a wise person? Perhaps someone who has these qualities:

Thoughtful and reflective. Wise people take life's experiences and reflect on the lesson in the long view. Something can be learned from every experience. Wise people use their reflections to help others see things differently, too. Can you quiet the noise in your brain to create room for learning? You don't need candles and spa music.

- Take a walk or immerse yourself in an activity that will focus you in a way that allows wisdom to emerge.
- Develop a habit of asking yourself a question at bedtime: "What did I learn today?"
- Use the "rule of ten" to gain perspective: What impact will this event/problem/decision have in ten minutes? Ten weeks? Ten months? Ten years?

"We are made wise not by the recollections of our past, but by the responsibilities of our future."

—George Bernard Shaw

Responsible. Shaw's wisdom offers a different take: While wisdom grows from reflection on the past, we can't simply rest on that reflection. Wisdom is about taking action, even when—perhaps especially when—we are not the direct beneficiaries of that action. Are you invested in a cause that is bigger than your day-to-day life? What is important enough to force you to go broader and deeper in your leadership involvement?

Compassionate. Compassion is essential to wisdom. It is the ability to put yourself in someone else's shoes and the willingness to act to address suffering. If you are able to lighten the load of others but do not act, ego overrules wisdom. Wisdom is not sedentary. The compassion required for wisdom is like a muscle that atrophies when it is not used. Many practices can keep your compassion toned up. A quick one is the "just like me" practice, developed by Leo Babauta (2017), the author of the *Zen Habits* blog. When someone pushes your buttons and makes it hard to feel compassion, try thinking about how that person is just like you. Maybe you think, "just like me, this person wants to be right," or "just like me, this person wants things to go well." Try it first with someone who is not your nemesis! This practice reminds us that we are often more connected with others than we recognize; that realization is a bridge to compassion.

"Humility [is] not thinking less of ourselves but thinking of ourselves less."

—Rick Warren

Humble. If you say you are wise, are you? Wisdom is a high bar. We probably are not as wise as we can be until the day we die. Do you have opportunities to show humility by deferring decisions to others rather than always needing to be in control? Do you have a habit of gratitude? Are there opportunities to show appreciation for the things that others do that make it possible for you to do what you do?

Genuine and imperfect. Wise people don't try to fool others, and they will admit they are sometimes foolish. We are awed when children say incredibly wise things; their wisdom shines through in the genuineness of their communication. They are not doing "impression management" or trying to *make* people see them as wise.

They immerse their whole selves into figuring things out. Listening well allows wisdom to come through; worrying about how we will be perceived or trying to be perfect does not. Admitting our imperfections makes us human, approachable, and real.

Able to read people. Reading people requires emotional intelligence, or the ability to scan a situation and take the emotional temperature while maintaining your own balance. The irony of this skill is that it requires you to give up preconceived notions of people to truly observe them. Practice setting aside your beliefs about someone, and instead note objectively what their body language, tone of voice, and facial expressions are telling you.

2. LEADERSHIP QUOTES AND QUESTIONS

Do you need a thought for the day to help you focus on being the best leader you can be today? So many great leaders have powerful words to offer. This section includes a selection of quotes to help you through today and reflections to support you in incorporating the messages into your actions and words *today.*

Words live on when they ring true for many people. Following each quote, you'll find questions to help you see what these leadership "pearls" might look like for you.

"Effective leaders don't have to be passionate. They don't have to be charming. They don't have to be brilliant. . . . What they must be is clear."

—Marcus Buckingham

- Do you struggle to make your expectations clear to employees? Try wrapping up a discussion with an employee by asking, "Before you go, I'd like you to tell me how you understand what we have agreed to."
- In speaking to a group, practice summarizing your desired result in one sentence; start with that before getting into the details.
- Join me in the quest to simplify! Sometimes we make things so complicated. Think about the message you want to deliver and how you would explain it to someone who knows nothing about it.

"Something special must leave the room when you leave the room."
—Attributed to Peter Drucker

- What is your "something special"—be honest, everyone has something to bring to the table. Do you bring humor? A balanced perspective? An eye for the downsides of ideas? An awareness of the effect of actions on morale? A historical view? Fresh eyes? Decisiveness? Optimism? Attention to detail?
- Whatever your gift, make it your goal to bring it to the table. Don't hide your talents. Even if you create some conflict, having a diversity of perspectives on a team will make it richer.
- Not sure what you bring to the mix? Ask your manager or peers what would be missing on the team if you weren't there.

"It is better to lead from behind and to put others in front, especially when you celebrate victory, when nice things occur. You take the front line when there is danger. Then people will appreciate your leadership."

—Nelson Mandela

- How do you elevate others? Take opportunities to recognize your employees' contributions to someone in a senior role at your organization or in your community.
- When you receive recognition, remember to mention those who helped you succeed and their specific contributions.
- People like to know that someone is keeping the alligators at bay. Work on establishing a reputation as someone who is always there, who goes the extra mile, who anticipates and addresses problems.

"The greatest mistake you can make in life is to be continually fearing you will make one."

—Elbert Hubbard

- If you thought you could do something (instead of assuming otherwise), what might you start?
- Then go ahead, do or try it! Talk about what you learned, especially if it did not go as planned. It is a gift to learn from our mistakes (which makes us better) and end the guilt and shame of failure (which zaps energy and produces nothing).
- Our integrity is undermined when we tell others that it is alright to make mistakes but then beat ourselves up for doing so. (Ironically, I had to face this music just minutes after writing this. Someone brought a mistake that I had made to my attention. I wanted to wallow in self-pity, but I decided to take my own advice, so I stopped to think about what I could learn from this mistake and how I could prevent it from happening again.)

"Let us make our future now, and let us make our dreams tomorrow's reality."

—Malala Yousafzai

- Write down three adjectives that you would like others to use five years from now to describe your leadership.
- What do you need to do *now* to make sure that is how you will be described? Connect your actions to those adjectives *every day*. Do you remember your third-grade teacher? I'll bet you could come up with a few adjectives. Good or bad, our actions leave a lasting impression.

"Write your own leadership quote."

- What is true about leadership, in your view? Find a statement that you believe in—or write your own—and post it in a place where you can see it and think about it frequently.

3. ENVISIONING SUCCESS

How do you imagine your best self? Are you in a rut and need inspiration to visualize what is possible for you? This section offers probing questions that will help you think about what you want for your future, which is the first step in making it come to life.

Your imagination is like a movie preview of your future, and the brain is an amazing thing. We can believe what we visualize as well as what we actually see before us. For this reason, it is important to be intentional about the pictures you put into your brain!

At the end of the year, or at anytime during the year, try to picture your life 12 months out. What do you hope for? How could you begin to create a vision for your success? Spend a few minutes thinking about the following questions *before* setting your goals for the next year, and you're more likely to achieve them.

What do you want your career to look like in the coming year? Imagine what you will be doing, how you will come across to others, what it will feel like, and what you would like to be able to say. What would you like to achieve, overcome, learn, or conquer?

What are three outstanding things you accomplished in the past 12 months? Think of things that were a stretch for you. If nothing big comes to mind, ask others to help you review the year's accomplishments. If you can't recall anything outstanding, perhaps now is the time to nudge yourself a bit.

Conduct your own personal SWOT analysis. SWOT—strengths, weaknesses, opportunities, and threats—analysis is a tool that is regularly used in organizational strategic planning to help organizations keep their eyes and ears attuned to the business environment (Gurel 2017). Use it to create a personal strategic plan that considers the influences in your environment.

- **List three personal strengths.** Strengths are the attributes that get you through difficult times, the personal resources that you draw on to grow, and the characteristics that are common to your success stories. A great book that will help you assess your strength is *Strengths Finders 2.0* by Tom Rath (2007). The University of Pennsylvania Arts and Sciences Positive Psychology Center, as part of a research project, also offers a strengths assessment. You can search for its free strengths test online.

- **List three weaknesses.** Whether we call them weaknesses or opportunities, we all have things to work on. Use this list to determine how well you are compensating for (e.g., by surrounding yourself with people who have qualities that you lack) or working to fix your weaknesses.

- **List three opportunities for the coming year.** Think about your vision for your career a year from now. What opportunities can you identify to reach that vision? What stretch assignments can you can go after to steer yourself toward this course?
- **List three threats to your success.** What barriers or obstacles could get in the way of your success?

The general goal with SWOT is to maximize strengths and opportunities and plan to minimize weaknesses and threats. When you develop your goals, they can often come right out of this exercise.

Look through more than one lens. Consider:

- Who are my key customers?
- What would I like them to say about me 12 months from now?
- What can I teach others?
- What can I learn from others?

"I am a person who values _____." Fill in the blank. To find a list of values, search online for "values list" and print the list. First, circle all the values that seem significant to you. Then cross off three of the values you circled. And cross off three more. Then cross off three more, until you are left with only five values that you cannot live without. Being keenly aware of your key values helps when you are struggling to make a decision. These values provide guidance on what is right for you. When we make decisions based on our values, we are happier with our choices.

Let the answers to these strategic questions feed the creation of your SMART goals for the year. Identify the key words or phrases you came up with in this exercise and write them on sticky notes, make them your computer screen saver, and keep them in sight.

4. WHAT MAKES YOU COME ALIVE?

Do you know what you are best at? Do you know when you are working "in the flow" and bringing your best talents to bear? These are days when the clock is forgotten. So many people do not pause to find this out about themselves or their employees. This section explores ways to "bring it."

"Don't ask what the world needs; ask what makes you come alive, because what the world needs is people who have come alive."

—Howard Thurman

I heard a family physician quote Thurman in a presentation about why he loved his rural medical practice. It prompted the question, "When I am at work, when do I feel most alive?" I know exactly when this happens for me.

Do you? Think of times when you have felt energized, well suited to your work, enthusiastic, inspired, and accomplished—when you have felt that "this work is a good fit for my talents."

Make a list—on paper or in your mind—of the tasks and projects that make you feel alive. How could you incorporate more of these things into your work?

What about your employees? Make a list of the ways your employees might answer this question. If you don't know, *ask*. Use this question as an opportunity for growth and connection.

For example, you could ask, "I'm interested in learning about the parts of your job that make you feel most enthusiastic, about the days you go home and feel like you had a really good day at work. When you have those days, what is it about the job that makes you feel that way?" Use their responses to brainstorm ways to build on their natural talents with new projects, to best use their energies and talents.

If your employees have a hard time answering the question, ask some follow-up questions: "Can you imagine a workday that would make you feel energized? For some people, it might be a lot of (or a little) patient or customer interaction. For others, it might be working with details and making them all come out right, working in teams, working alone, or perhaps coming up with new ways of doing things. For still others, it might be crossing a lot of tasks off their to-do list. Do any of these ring a bell with you?" This dialogue can help you learn about an individual's talents, make employees feel valued, and energize them to come up with some new ideas for their work.

Does it make your day when someone you have mentored is successful? Are you inspired by helping someone turn their natural talents into great performance? You know this feeling when it hits you—it is the opposite of envy. You feel proud of the person who has achieved a goal that you coached them through. Everyone wins when this happens.

This desire to coach and to help others grow may or may not come naturally to you, but coaching skills and processes can be learned. You can retain good employees when you help bring out their natural talents toward a useful goal.

Matching the right work to the right people is a leadership talent to hone not only for your employees' success but your own. The feeling of fulfillment that you get when someone you have coached or mentored does well is the essence of coaching.

5. LEADING? GO!

Do you need inspiration right this minute? Find it in this section.

Leadership starts this minute. Yes, it is a long-view proposition involving strategic thinking, deliberation, and time carved out for work that isn't urgent. But it has to start somewhere. Here are some things you can do today—right now—that will pay long-term dividends:

Your efficiency. Before you leave work today, make a list of tomorrow's priorities. When you come in tomorrow, reflect on how this simple practice made you feel. Was it a little easier to transition to your personal time and avoid spending your energy trying not to forget things? Did you feel a sense of "lightness" as you committed actions from your mind onto a paper or electronic list?

A new collaboration. Ask someone who knows you well to write five quick tips on how best to work with you—your quirks, your communication style, your sense of humor (or lack thereof), the best way to approach you, and so on. Share this list with a new colleague to help build your relationship on a strong foundation.

Your workplace culture. Walk around your building, say hello to everyone you meet, smile, and make eye contact. Have a handful of open-ended questions in mind to show interest in what people are working on.

That employee—you know the one. Strike up a conversation about the person's work, their day, or what is currently challenging them. We tend to avoid people we don't necessarily like or feel comfortable around, but sometimes when we actually sit down and talk, we find that it is not as difficult as we expected. Even if it still is awkward, push yourself to interact, inquire, and listen. It is an investment in a relationship that you may need in the future.

Your civic engagement. Spend five minutes finding the names and contact information for your elected officials and file it in an easy-to-access place. Write a quick email to one of them today to thank them for serving and to let them know you will be in touch throughout their term to share ideas on topics that are important to you.

Your self-esteem. The best way to boost your self-esteem is to *do the hard thing*. What have you been avoiding? Is there a discussion you need to have that you have been postponing, fearing it won't go well? A project that you are unsure how to start? If you wait until you are confident in taking action, you may be waiting a long time. Simply *begin*. Talk to the person you need to talk to. Write down the first three actions you need to take to start a daunting project. By breaking a difficult task or project into doable action steps, you will build confidence *and* motivation, which, in turn, build self-esteem.

Your reputation. Leave your phone behind when you attend meetings today. Like it or not, when you use your phone during meetings, it says to the people present, "You are not important to me." Is that the message you want to send?

Your health. Don't start an exercise and healthy eating *program*. The problem with programs is that they usually start in the future. Just get up and move now. Walk around the building for 10 minutes right now. If someone asks to talk to you for a few minutes, walk and talk at the same time. Make your next food choice a vegetable. Leave all the good parking places for someone else and park in the farthest spot from the entrance everywhere you drive today.

The environment. Do better than recycle: refuse. Role model stewardship by going plastic-free today. Drink water from the tap, out of a reusable glass, without a straw. For this day, do not contribute to the mountain of water bottles in landfills.

Team morale. Thank someone. Surely someone on your team has done something you appreciate. You might not have thought it deserved attention, but a little thank you pays dividends when you need to ask for help next time.

6. DAILY PEP TALKS

Are you having a difficult day? Does staying focused seem impossible? Be your own coach. This section provides guiding questions and reflections geared toward refocusing on your priorities.

"Life is difficult."

This first line of the classic, long-running best seller by Scott Peck, *The Road Less Traveled* (1978), has stayed with me for decades. "Life is difficult" has certainly stood the test of time. It is impossible to miss the angst we are experiencing as a nation, as people are divided in their beliefs and positions on just about every issue. While it is important to look and strive for the best, expecting things to be easy and smooth can set us up for struggle.

As a leader, you know that things do not always go according to plan. In those moments, how do we rise above the difficulties when disappointments and challenges are inevitable? You have to be a good coach to yourself as well as your team. There are many roads. The following are a few ways to build in daily coaching "pep talks" for yourself to boost your personal leadership and manage what is difficult for you.

Put your values into action. If you have not already narrowed down your values to your top five, do that first (find a plan for this in the section "Visualize Success"). This part is about clearly identifying actions that demonstrate your top five values and bringing them to life. *Daily pep talk:* Today I will focus on the value of _____. One thing I will do to reveal the importance of this value to me and help me feel I am walking the talk is _____.

Practice. If you have ever learned to play a musical instrument, you remember that your first attempt didn't sound great. You had to practice. So remember, when we call something "practice," it means to *practice*, not to be perfect at it. For example, a meditation practice requires some effort. Instead of insisting that you can't meditate because you tried once in 2010 and couldn't do it, try practicing it again. And then again. Over time, meditative breathing becomes a way to course-correct throughout the day when difficulties arise. *Daily pep talk:* Today I am going to practice _____ (e.g., meditation, five grounding breaths, mindful eating, relaxing my shoulders every time I wash my hands, etc.)

Identify your bright lights. Who are the touchstones, your go-to sources of comfort and support? We all need them, and we all have the opportunity to be them for someone else. *Daily pep talk:* Today I am going to look out for someone who makes me laugh and someone who makes me think. I will stop what I am doing and let their energy boost me. I will turn around and give that energy to someone else who needs it.

Look to nature. Don't wait for springtime to get outside and enjoy some fresh air. Stale air, stale thoughts. Literally breathe new life into solutions for your challenges. Nature is the antidote to our online addiction. Take a break from the news and noise and force yourself into the open air. *Daily pep talk:* Today I will find opportunities to move outside and notice the nature around me. I will have at least one ten-minute walking meeting/discussion with a colleague.

Use the buddy system. Who could give you a different perspective? Seek out a person who will nudge you to see things differently rather than a person who will just agree with you. It may even be someone who irritates you a little bit! *Daily pep talk:* Today I will pause to talk with someone who sees things differently than I do. I will ask them to push back on my statements and ask me for data to support my perceptions.

Keep it simple. Every day, do one good thing for your body. Read something that is uplifting. Get rid of one thing that clutters your life. Laugh and make someone else laugh. Stimulate your mind with a book, a conversation, or a daydream. *Daily pep talk:* Today I will do one thing on this list!

7. REFLECTIONS ON CEO GEMS

Do you wonder what is on the minds of successful and well-respected leaders around you? This section includes reflections from several CEOs on what helps them stay focused in a world of distractions. These wise leaders share some pearls of wisdom for moving from flustered chaos to calm determination.

A panel of successful and highly respected rural hospital CEOs in Wisconsin spoke to a group of new healthcare leaders during a May 2019 Rural Wisconsin Health Cooperative Leadership Residency. The pearls of wisdom that I gleaned from them may not surprise you, but they are wonderful reminders for reflecting on how to inspire leadership. Use the reflection questions after each one to consider how you exhibit these qualities.

- If you want people to understand you, speak to their minds. If you want people to follow you, speak to their hearts. *What is the employee's emotional side of an issue on which you want buy-in?*
- Be OK with course correction. *When things don't go as planned, how do you show that you can go with the flow?*
- Say regularly, "We are good at change." *What if you talked about change this way instead of saying that change is hard?*

- Develop a new peer network for support and learning. *Who in your leadership peer group have you reached out to for mutual support?*

- As a CEO, you are thinking about three years from now rather than about today's problems. *How much of today's work is focused on the future rather than what is on fire now?*

- Admit when you are wrong. *What might stop you from doing this?*

- Surround yourself with great people, with a diversity of strengths. *Do you encourage people to use their best talents, even if that means letting go of some control and credit?*

- Never burn a bridge. *How are you doing at letting go and keeping the door open?*

- Raise your hand to new opportunities, even if you have no experience. *What opportunity scares you? Sign up for it!*

- Be transparent. *What steps can you take to build more trust to encourage transparency?*

- Let go of having to be right. Focus instead on what is getting results. *How might your need to be right get in the way of your effectiveness?*

- Be a continuous learner. *What is the last book, class, or conversation that made you think hard about your leadership? What is your next learning goal?*

- "Don't tear down the fence until you know why the fence was built." *Do you regularly build inquiry into your decision-making?*

- Hire people you want to invest in, then invest in them. *Are you coaching people in a way that you could go on vacation and things would go well without you? How about coaching them to surpass you?*

- People are watching you and will take your lead. Lead by example. *What actions have you taken in the last hour that you would want others to emulate?*

- Be introspective about outcomes you do and do not achieve. Develop a habit of reflecting on what went well and what could be better. *If introspection is not in your nature, could you add it to your calendar as a five-minute task?*

- Care. People are attracted to people who care. *What do you care about?*

- Remember that when you are the leader, you are more like the orchestra conductor than the clarinet player, even if the clarinet is your individual talent. It's about getting the whole orchestra playing well together rather than zeroing in on one instrument. *Even if you are a working manager, how do you show that you see the bigger picture?*

- Communicate the "why." *Pick a current initiative and have a conversation with an employee about why it matters.*

- Make rounds with people and ask regularly, "What can I do to be more effective as a leader?" *How do you ask this in a way that makes it safe for people to respond honestly?*

- The only thing you have at the end of the day is your integrity. Make sure you don't sacrifice it for what is easier in short-term hardships. Do what is right, not what is easy. *Who or what helps you sort out sticky situations?*

- Learn from the bad leaders, too. *Who taught you what not to do, and what did you learn?*

- Hire tough, manage easy. Filling a position with a warm body will most likely become your biggest problem. *Do you keep your team involved and informed about hard-to-fill openings and recognize them for their extra efforts until you find the right fit?*

- Your attitude is your choice on a daily basis. *What habits are you practicing to keep your attitude positive?*

- Be authentically you. You have to figure out your own way. *Who or what helps you maintain your perspective and keeps you from comparing yourself with others?*

- You have to figure out your own work life integration/balance. There are no exact rules for how to do this, but know that you do no good for others if you are not at your best. *What early symptoms tell you that you are not at your best? What are the signs that rebalancing is needed?*
- IT'S ALL ABOUT RELATIONSHIPS. *What relationships need a greater investment?*

CHAPTER 3

Work Habits

OUR DAILY ACTIONS add up to make us feel accomplished or deflated, energized or exhausted. You have more control over this than you might think. This chapter focuses on helping you become your own best supporter through the actions you take every day.

SELF-ASSESSMENT SCORING:

1—I am struggling with or not yet skilled at this.

2—I am starting to work on improving at this, but I need more skill building.

3—I am making some consistent progress in improving at this.

4—I am doing very well in this area.

Determine your current level of skill on these work habits competencies (score 1–4):

1. I take vacations and breaks that refuel me. Score: _____

2. I set regular reminders to do the things that matter most at the beginning of every day. Score: _____

3. I use consensus decision-making appropriately, and I know which circumstances call for it and which ones do not. Score: _____

4. I set boundaries on my life and manage myself well from day to day. Score: _____

5. I adapt easily to change. Score: _____

6. My attention is fully present in the moment. Score: _____

7. When things are ambiguous, I manage myself without anxiety. Score: _____

8. I avoid procrastination. Score: _____

9. I use an effective, systematic approach to hold myself and others accountable. Score: _____

10. My goals light a fire in me. Score: _____

11. I balance work and life effectively for my full enjoyment and feeling of achievement. Score: _____

Now explore the corresponding sections that follow to learn how to improve skills that need work or enhance your current skills.

1. VACATION!

When was the last time you enjoyed your time off? Do you want to address the barriers to getting away? Think about how much time you have left in your life and how you want to spend it—not just how you spend your limited number of days off, but also how you build in breaks during the day to refuel your energy and spirit.

Workers in the United States receive less than half the vacation time than is standard in most European countries, and increasingly we are guilty of not using the time we do have. Not me. I have never left a vacation day on the table—think of me what you will. In many ways, our baby-boomer-designed work culture rewards martyrdom, causing us to feel that we must "prove" our dedication to the workplace by never taking time off. Just by confessing that I use my vacation time, I run the risk that I will not be perceived as dedicated. This perception can cause people to neglect the work-life balance that most leaders I have worked with say they desire. Many people find it simpler to avoid taking a vacation. Here are some of the reasons:

- **The pile.** Thinking about all the work we will come back to after a vacation makes us already feel tired for tomorrow, so we skip resting, believing we'll be punished for it.
- **I *have* to be there.** We believe no one else can cover for us, that missed meetings are too important. Sometimes this is true, but are there alternatives that go unexamined? Could it be tied to the next question . . .
- **What if they realize they don't need me?** There is a fear: I can't relax or I will lose everything.

But when we neglect our vacations, what does it say to the people we lead? Jim Loehr and Tony Schwartz share research from their work in *The Power of Full Engagement* (2003, 4) showing that we don't get more done by staying at work longer and refusing to take breaks: "Energy, not time, is the fundamental currency of high performance." Giving our all when we *are* at work is what matters most. We do that best when we are rested.

The following are examples of how leaders show support for work-life balance—for yourself and for your team:

- **Avoid scheduling meetings on Mondays mornings and Friday afternoons.** This allows people to take long weekends more easily.

- **Take a break from mandatory meetings in July and December** if they are not mission critical. It's not a work stoppage—just an opportunity in the summer and winter for people to feel more freedom to be off work. It might even build in more enthusiasm for teams to have a break from meetings.

- **Incorporate time off into your productivity models.** If you don't, what you are really saying is that people can take time off, but they will have to work twice as hard before and after vacation. That's not rest.

- **Plan for succession and delegate well.** Develop others so you can trust them to take the wheel. If your presence is so important that you can't take a break, you may need to refocus your efforts on these two leadership responsibilities.

- **Lead by example.** If a leader says "Take your time off, we support work-life balance here" but works through their own vacations, employees hear "Don't take a break."

- **Build teamwork.** Strong teams who care about each other as people *want* to cover for their coworkers. Asking for help demonstrates that your team can ask for help when they need it, too.

Although a long vacation is great, our daily habits pack as big a punch when it comes to staying at the top of our game. Do you build in restful (whatever restful means to *you*) weekends and evenings throughout the week? Do you take mini-breaks during the work day, including a nutrition break and maybe a quick walk?

If you are fortunate to love your work, as I do, the lines between work and nonwork time can easily become blurry. But what else do you love? When is the last time you were able to fully enjoy doing those things and leave work at work?

Remember: we are all mortal. Right now, write a list of five things you want to do before you die. Keep it where you can see it, and start doing those things.

"You know all those things you always wanted to do? You should go and do them."

—E. J. Lamprey

---

2. WORD GAMES: DAILY REMINDERS FOR A PRIORITIZED WORKWEEK

Would some simple reminders help you prioritize tasks that might otherwise fall to the bottom of the pile? This section offers a few ideas to get you started.

When the day-to-day fires start to blaze, it helps to have a structure to keep what is most important top of mind. Try coming up with a few word games to remind yourself what matters most every day. Word association might seem too simple to be useful, but that's the beauty of it. Think of these alliterations as anchors for keeping your priorities straight. Consider the following ideas (or come up with your own) to set up a focused work week:

Margin Monday. Strategic thinking is a leadership competency. Back-to-back meetings and appointments do not allow for this kind of contemplation. "Margin" refers to scheduling space in your calendar for strategic thinking. Set aside time to plan, think, prepare, and organize your work intentionally—no one else is going to do this for you. Propose a policy of no-meeting Mondays, or at least not in the mornings. Use Monday to identify priorities for the week, check in with your team on their goals, and learn what support they need from you. **Alternative: Metric Monday.** What data do you need each week to make sure that your department is on track? Identify a couple of key data points (productivity, patient or customer satisfaction, overtime, expenses) that you will check every Monday.

Trouble Tuesday. I once heard a speaker say to a group of leaders, "Don't run *from* trouble, run *to* it." Is there something you have been putting off because you have concerns or don't feel confident about how to tackle it? A difficult conversation you need to have? A can of worms that needs to be opened? Make Tuesday the day to look trouble in the eye and face unpleasant challenges.

Wellness Wednesday. Has half the week gone by and you haven't built in any time for your own health? Have you been skipping lunch, not taking breaks, or holding your breath due to stress? Schedule time on Wednesday for your own wellness, and you will be a role model for your employees. **Alternative: Why Wednesday.** This replaces the old favorite "hump day" with a reminder that understanding the "why" behind our work increases people's engagement.

Thank You Thursday. Who do you need to thank? Do you appreciate people in your head but neglect to tell them out loud? Who is going the extra mile? Who has come up with a new idea or solved a problem this week? Thanking people for a specific effort reinforces desired behaviors. If an employee has had performance problems in the past and overcome them, acknowledge the change. Give attention to your high performers—especially if you want to keep them.

Fun Friday. We might not need to be reminded about TGIF, but how do you have fun at work? Healthcare, like many workplace environments, is serious, but we need not always be solemn. When we are laughing, we are learning.

A sense of humor is a lifesaver when we are facing a heavy workload and the pressure is on. What tone do you set with your body language and facial expression that gives—or takes away—permission to have a little fun? Look in the mirror. Be intentional about the messages you communicate and bring some lightness to your work environment.

3. CONSENSUS DECISION-MAKING

> **Do you feel like decisions that should be easy get bogged down, taking too much time and energy? Alternatively, are some decisions made hastily, leaving key stakeholders without a chance to have a say?** Consensus is a crucial skill when it is the *right* decision-making style, but it can exhaust precious resources when it is overused. Read this section to determine when consensus is and is not the right way to make a decision.

In healthcare, it seems we have a "consensus" about consensus. The norm is, "Let's get everyone's ideas, make sure you all get a chance to have your say, and then we will discuss the merits and challenges of each idea until we can agree on the best decision." Consensus doesn't mean that everyone gets what they want; rather, after a thorough discussion, everyone consents to the outcome and walks out the door with a shared understanding. At its best, consensus is a powerful process that builds buy-in because people feel heard. It can prevent unintended consequences because all stakeholders weigh in. Consensus also can help people relate to the bigger picture, because the decision is aimed at the greater good rather than an individual point of view.

Consider, though, that consensus is not the *best* decision-making process, it is just one of many decision-making processes.

Here are some pitfalls of consensus decision-making and strategies for improvement:

Overuse. Where should we go for lunch? Should we choose the tan or the brown tile for the mail room? Should we lock the crash cart? We often have long, drawn-out discussions about choices that are best made by a simple majority vote or assignment of a delegate to decide, or decisions that are governed by a regulation that overrides all discussion anyway!

- To keep your team's energy high, save consensus for decisions that have high impact and that are not driven by forces beyond your control.

Underuse. Some leaders adopt an authoritarian decision-making style, believing that consensus takes too much time. People check out because there is no opportunity for them to engage in the conversation, and they feel like their voice is not heard.

- Develop your facilitation skills to encourage discussion and learn to focus on *process* as well as *outcome*.

Midwestern niceness. This may explain some of the enthusiasm for consensus where I come from, and maybe it's not just the Midwest. It is "polite" to give everyone the chance to speak their views, and we believe we "ought to." However, even though we may offer the opportunity, that same "niceness" can keep people from openly disagreeing. People nod their heads and you think, "Great! We have consensus!" But what you may have instead is compliance (at best). This compliance is actually a false consensus which can stall your change efforts leaving you wondering how something that seemed so agreeable is not moving forward. It is also a perfect setup for the "meeting after the meeting," a real energy drainer in which employees say all the things that were not said openly, leaving grudges to fester. Go for robust disagreement that is carried on openly and respectfully. To work toward true consensus:

- Invite people to disagree, and then thank them when they do so.
- Attend to your team's relationships in *other* ways, so that people feel safe expressing unpopular views.
- Establish participation agreements (or ground rules) that encourage respectful disagreement, and then follow them.

Fear of taking charge. You are the leader, and it is alright to make unilateral decisions about some things. If you tend to shy away from decisiveness, fearing that you will come across like a dictator, consensus can feel like you are doing the right thing, when in fact you might be exhausting yourself and your team unnecessarily.

- If a decision is nonnegotiable, make the decision and inform the team. Don't waste their time discussing something that you have already decided and for good reason.
- Explain your decision-making process and the reasoning behind it. For example, "I will make the decisions on this event because time is critical and I need your energy focused on developing our long-term plans," or "majority will rule, so let's vote," or "we need consensus on this because it is important and will affect everyone so I need your honest thoughts and best ideas. This may take some time but in the end we will come out with a decision that we can all get behind."
- Build trust with your team so they know if you make a decision without asking their input, they are more likely to assume good intent on your part.
- Get comfortable with not making everyone happy. When you do the right thing, it does not always end in happiness, but you can make it end with integrity.

4. MANAGING YOU

Does it seem like you are managing departments, budgets, and workloads, but when it comes to managing your own day, it is a little chaotic? Habits can help, and good managing starts with managing yourself. This section shares some easy-to-apply boundaries that can change the shape of your daily experience for the better.

Many books have been written on the distinction between management and leadership. However you define these concepts, both are important and necessary. Both also have ever-evolving best practices, and as managers and leaders (titled or not), we must be ever-evolving. If we don't grow, we risk becoming obsolete and unable to attract and keep an excellent workforce—a workforce that is also constantly changing.

Management may not be as "exciting" as leadership, but without good management, chaos reigns. We need both to be successful at our change efforts. If you have ever followed a leader who lacked management resources and skills, it may have felt as if you were taking flight without wings and fuel, flight plan, or clear destination. Working for a manager without leadership abilities feels like you are never allowed to get off the tarmac, because you are so bogged down by the details and "what ifs" and waiting for 100 percent certainty. There is a natural tension between leadership and management. When we get the balance right, it is like nature's elements of earth, fire, water and air all sustaining life (versus earthquakes, raging fires, floods, and cyclones that destroy).

Start by considering how effectively you are managing *you*. Before you can manage a group of people, you must first look at your own projects and workload. If you are too frequently overwhelmed, missing deadlines, or can't find what you are looking for, it's time to put some systems in place for yourself. Some simple time and energy management techniques can help:

- **Know your peak time.** Figure out when you do your best work and schedule your most mentally challenging tasks during that time.

- **Unapologetically build in planning time.** If you don't have structured planning time on your calendar, start with a regular half hour on the first and last day of your workweek for big-picture plans and just a few minutes at the beginning and end of each day for today's and tomorrow's plans. Be unapologetic in claiming time for this, even in the face of demands from others. When we move from individual contributor to manager, planning feels like we are not "producing," and many managers are not comfortable with this. Planning effectively is a task of a manager. Claim it and put it on your list. Not only is it important to spend dedicated planning time, but also you model for others that this is a valued practice that you support for them as well.

- **Limit meetings to 45 minutes.** Shorter is fine, too! If you typically schedule one-hour meetings, back to back, after the first hour you are running late all day. If meeting times are not your call, ask for organizational support for this idea to give everyone time to recalibrate between meetings (the asking shows leadership). This allows for physical health benefits, too: We move, we get to go to the restroom, get a glass of water—all things that we sacrifice when we run late.

Get familiar with key data points about your work. Data is your friend, even if you are not a numbers person—actually, *especially* if you are not a numbers person. What are the major drivers of success for your projects and staff? Once your leadership vision defines where you are headed, identify the top two or three numbers that will tell you if you are on the right track. If you learn and know the top two or three numbers, you can make course corrections faster, and you will be paying attention to the most important things when time is limited.

Establish rituals. Much like families in chaos, having something that you can count on in times of change can build resilience by managing what you *can* manage. Some teams have a structured "huddle" at the start of the day to connect actions to purpose. Great teams build in and commit to regular recognition of each other at the beginning of every team meeting as a way of actively creating a culture of appreciation. What rituals can you build into your work that will help you manage yourself and your team?

5. ADAPT

Do you struggle when things change or don't turn out as planned? Do you fail to make a commitment because you are too adaptable, leaving people unsure of what the goal is? Turn to this section and explore ways to strengthen your adaptability muscle and reflect on when you might need to be less adaptable to lead clearly.

Adaptability is one of the most sought-after qualities in a leader. In my experience, being inflexible, even if you are technically talented, derails more careers than any other issue. Think about the last time things did not go as planned or a change occurred that you did not care for. How did you respond? Do you "go to the mat" for things to be done the old way?

Although survival depends on adaptability, the brain fights us on adaptation. The brain likes getting into a groove—that is why developing habits helps us do things we might not always feel like doing (such as working out or getting up early). But habits can also put us on autopilot, causing us to overlook new ways of solving problems. It's worth developing your mental agility muscle.

Instead of responding "That's wrong," try "That's different." This small change keeps your mind's door from slamming shut. It offers you a chance to listen and learn. You don't have to *speak* the words "that's wrong" to believe it yourself, or for others to believe your body language that says so.

Become an early adopter. Is it possible that you have already earned a reputation as inflexible? Find something new to learn about (the latest gadget, a function of electronic medical record that no one else knows about) and learn all about it. Offer to share what you have learned with others to show them that you are willing to learn, and they will be more likely to keep you in the communication loop in the future. A pitfall of being seen as a resister is that people avoid telling you about changes because they dread hearing, "That will never work," "We tried that years ago," or "Why fix what isn't broken." This information vacuum feeds your reputation and creates a vicious cycle for you. Break it.

Try something new every day. Tie your shoes with the opposite loop first, park in a different spot, or work in a different location. Flip a meeting agenda from bottom to top. These are small actions, but they build your capacity for adaptability. This skill will come in handy when weightier issues require you to be more open minded.

Work on your perception that change is difficult. Our ability to adapt (or lack thereof) shows up most in times of change. "When life settles down, we'll be able to _____ (fill in the blank)." We hold our breath and tighten our muscles through change, just waiting for comfort. Adaptability is working toward getting comfortable *during* the change. Examine this belief by looking back on past changes that turned out fine. How much time and energy did you spend struggling? What did you miss? How might you have spent that energy differently if you had known it would all eventually be alright?

If you are digging in your heels, consider that you might be experiencing fear. Fear is perfectly normal, but many of us hide it. Fear is often playing out behind the scenes as we push back against a perceived loss. Mitigate the fear of loss by addressing it directly:

- Loss of feeling competent—address with skill building. No one wants to look incompetent.
- Loss of status, belonging, your "place" in the organization—reach out to others to build new relationships. People want to know where they fit in.
- Loss of freedom to do things your way or the way that works for you—ask for dialogue about ideas; ask to share *your* ideas and discuss alternatives. People want a say in things that affect them. It is empowering.
- Loss of certainty—certainty is a myth, so identify what you *can* control. The "Serenity Prayer" fits here: Ask for "the serenity to accept the things I cannot change, the courage to change the things I can, and the wisdom to know the difference." It fits in addiction recovery, and it fits in becoming more adaptable to change in the workplace.

On the other hand, can you be too adaptable? Here are some signs that you may be overflexing:

Others perceive you (or you perceive yourself) as wishy-washy. Sometimes what looks like flexibility is really people pleasing. If so, welcome to the club. Examine your motives and find a different club to join. We cannot please everyone, and it is important to realize this sooner rather than later. It's exhausting and short-sighted. Keep your ultimate goal in sight.

You do not feel confident. It takes confidence to be an effective leader, but confidence is a journey with ups and downs. Self-doubt is natural when you are new to a role, you have new or greater responsibilities, or you don't have training in an area that you must now lead. Self-doubt may leave you swaying in whatever wind is blowing the strongest. Find a mentor who can help you crystallize a vision of where you are headed. The details may have to be flexible, but a clear destination will give you a North Star to guide the way.

6. BE HERE NOW

Is your mind in the past or future rather than the present moment? Do your employees feel like you are not really "there" for them because your mind is elsewhere? Distractions can keep us from experiencing the present moment and affect your leadership presence. This section offers practical tips for showing up where you are and why it matters.

Presence matters. Thirty years ago, I was seeing a doctor for a recurring problem that just would not get better. Every time I talked with him, he was looking at charts, washing his hands, talking with the nurse—always doing several things at once. One day he came in and I had not put on my gown for the exam. He started to leave, saying he'd be back when I was ready. I said, "No. I am not going to say or do anything until you sit down and look at me and listen to me!" We started making progress that day.

Young people may be able to multi-task better than most of us—the jury is still out on that. Even if so, evolution doesn't happen overnight. Much of the time, we have to toggle from one task to the next and back again, trying not to lose our momentum. Most of us could do a better job of being fully present, being in one place at a time, and tuning in when it matters. When we try to juggle multiple tasks that each require mental concentration, we fail to do any of them well. Look at the statistics for texting and driving for all the evidence you need to prove this point.

We help ourselves when we are fully present because we get more done, with better results. Our employees and peers benefit by feeling respected and appreciated, which increases employee engagement. Like my own story illustrates, even patients get better quicker when we give them our full attention.

Consider the following ideas to improve your concentration and results:

Decide. Consciously, with intention and thought, make a decision to do one thing at a time. If you are not going to pay attention to the phone conference, hang up. If you are not going to listen at the staff meeting, don't go. If you don't like the consequences of those decisions and must participate even though you don't want to, decide to listen and ask questions. Here is a question for you: Is actively deciding something you could do more of? We forget that we can make conscious decisions instead of passive ones about many things—even if the decision is simply how we will respond.

Take responsibility for boredom. Confession: Sometimes I check my emails or texts during a boring webinar. A courageous alternative is to speak up about being bored. What if, instead of checking out mentally by layering another task, say or write in the chat feature, "I am trying but I am not connecting to this presentation right now. I wonder if you could talk a little bit more about how this applies to our work, give a real life example or story, address something I am very curious about, answer this question, etc." This takes guts. Consider, though, that you may not be the only one who is bored. Speaking up respectfully can help you and others engage more fully and create a better outcome.

Use your body to help you. Sit on your hands. Lean in toward the speaker. Put down your phone, pen, or notebook. Sit squarely facing the work you are choosing. Turn toward anyone who is speaking. Sit up and take a deep breath.

Out of sight, out of mind. When you are driving, put your phone out of reach so you won't be tempted to look at it. Close your email when you are on a phone conference. Close open files. Remove other work from your visual, auditory, and other sensory radar so that you will be less distracted.

Find a tactile assist. If you can't sit still and must be doing something, choose a task that does not require mental concentration. Stand, pace, doodle, or play with a desk toy. Sometimes I knit in meetings, an activity that is very easy for me and requires no thought at all. My mental energy stays focused on the discussion, but my hands don't go looking for something else to do that will distract me.

Spend one minute thinking. Before you start to layer tasks, ask yourself what you really want to accomplish in one hour (or whatever time constraint you are facing). At the end of that hour, what goal do you want to have achieved? This technique can help you focus your time and take charge of your energy.

7. AMBIGUITY

Are you dissatisfied when you haven't crossed many items off your to-do list at the end of the day, even though you worked hard? Is the longing for certainty something you did not anticipate when you wanted to become a leader? Getting comfortable with ambiguity is a skill that leaders must master. Read this section for specific ideas on how to increase your comfort level when certainty is not an option.

Leadership tip: Get more comfortable with ambiguity. Sit down and have a cup of coffee with it, snuggle up and be friends. Otherwise, ambiguity—a sense of uncertainty—will raise your anxiety or turn you into a control freak, interfering with your success. When you put in an IV, run a lab test, or fix a piece of machinery, you know when you are done. In a technical role, much of the work is unambiguous and thus satisfying to complete. In leadership roles, though, when you are coaching employees, improving the culture in your department, or becoming a more effective communicator, you never feel done. Confidence can slip because the clear markers of daily achievement have changed. This leads to a couple of traps:

- The trap of continuing to do the job from which you were promoted. Your old job may be more comfortable and make you feel competent, but you miss delegation opportunities and have less time to do leadership work.
- Ambiguity becomes overwhelming, and we either micromanage to regain a sense of control or we start to spin mentally. The result is a mess. Both overcontrolling and spinning eat up a lot of energy and time. We get behind on important things, and it becomes a vicious cycle.

In a sea of ambiguity, if we want to have a sense of achievement and confidence at the end of the workday, we have to redefine what brings us satisfaction and learn to function well with a higher level of uncertainty. Here are a few things you can do:

Control consciously. Ask yourself what you do and don't have control over. For the things you don't have control over (other people, decisions beyond your scope, the future), decide what you can and want to *influence*. Focus your efforts into what you can control (your own attitude, behavior, approach), which will help you wield that influence.

Break big goals into daily tasks. If, for example, you are working to improve the culture in your department, today's list might be: "Review culture survey scores and select two key markers to focus on." Tomorrow's list: "Spend 5 minutes writing down specific behaviors that would demonstrate those key markers." Each of the next three days: "Find one person in the department to recognize for those positive behaviors." Breaking big goals down into daily tasks helps keep overwhelm at bay, and you will see progress toward your larger goal.

Be a pioneer. Our brains love to be on autopilot: We drive the same route to work every day, eat the same foods, run our meetings the same way, and so on. Habits can be good things, but one way to expand our openness to the unknown is to change things up. Even little changes can make a difference because they remind us that not knowing is not fatal. Pioneers venture where there are no paths. Sometimes you may end up on a dead-end trail, but new territory is where discoveries are made.

Take risks. We would all perform perfectly if we had 100 percent of the data and skill needed for the task at hand. But a truer mark of a leader is the willingness to be innovative when you don't have 100 percent. If you are a perfectionist or have a tough time with corrective coaching or mistakes, practice making small decisions without having all the data you would like. All scientific discoveries start with the unknown. Be willing to sit with knowing that you don't know to remain open to what is possible and what might be learned. Remember, most people don't get fired for stepping up to try to improve things, even if it doesn't go as planned.

Practice mindfulness. When I asked my husband how he deals with ambiguity, he said, "I just focus on what is right in front of me; is that bad?" I laughed, because this is so true, and it is one of the best ways he influences me. You could call that denial, or you could look at it as mindfulness—*being fully present in the moment* instead of worrying about the future.

We are certain to have uncertainty. Managing it skillfully is like learning to let go of one trapeze bar and making the most of the moment *before* you catch the next one.

8. PROCRASTINATION

Do you procrastinate? A variety of needs underlie the procrastination habit. This section focuses on some common motivational needs and offers suggestions for overcoming procrastination.

What an evil beast! I've been doing it all morning, when I could have just gotten this writing done. I checked email compulsively and answered the easy unimportant ones, got some hot chocolate, cleaned up a couple of piles of paper on my desk, etc., etc.

You may know the drill . . .

Overwhelmed? Unpleasant task? Perfectionism? Not in the right mood? Know you can't get it done, so why start? Can't decide? These reasons boil down to feeling like you *can't* do it or *don't want to* do it. Important tasks don't just go away, do they? So, how can you get started?

One method for overcoming procrastination is to figure out what gets you out of "first gear" by identifying an unmet need. Depending on your personality type, some of the following tips may be helpful:

The need to take quick action. Do *anything*. Make a list of tasks so that you can cross them off as you go (the crossing off action feeds motivation for some people). Break a project into tiny chunks and complete *any* part of it—any feeling of accomplishment builds on itself. Do a part of a project quickly, even if you have to fix it later. Set a timer for 30 minutes and work on any part of the project for that amount of time. Chances are, you'll keep going because the "fire" will be started.

The need to have an influence. Call a friend—but with a purpose! Ask someone whom you look up to or admire what they would do with the project if it was theirs. Talk through how the project could benefit others or help someone else in the end. Feeling that your work will have a positive impact on others can provide a breath of fresh air to get you motivated.

The need to find the best way. Limit your options. This advice may sound counterintuitive, but when the options are endless, it's hard to land on one—hence the relentless search for the "very best" way. Pick *three* options (a way to do the project or resources to check, whatever defines your project) and select from only those three, and you will move toward accomplishment more quickly. It's like letting the particles in the water settle down so that you can clearly see the goal you are swimming toward.

The need to do it the right way. Spend some time putting the project in order. The project may seem huge and chaotic, and you can't get started until you have a plan. Find a quiet spot where you can't see your other work and give yourself a set time (30 minutes to one hour—but not days!). Start with a list of everything that needs to be done and then put the list in logical order. Once you feel you have applied some order, you can begin at A and move to Z. A sense of order can help you feel like there is solid ground beneath you. The need for order may be the most challenging obstacle to overcome, because there are endless details to consider, and you may be looking for the *one* right way. If this sounds like you, another idea is to make a list of all the things that could go wrong. For some folks, it feels better to think about the downsides first, to make sure nothing gets missed. If you want to be effective and reduce your stress, decide whether your plan can be "good enough" or whether it must be "perfect." For example, taking your turn typing up meeting minutes can be done "good enough"; completing ten employee reviews by a deadline must be done on time and thoughtfully, but they won't be perfect; eye surgery needs to be perfect. Pick your perfects.

Goal: Quit procrastinating . . . tomorrow? Just kidding. Start right now.

9. A SYSTEM FOR ACCOUNTABILITY

> **Could your team benefit from a system that would show their work progress in real time? Do you have to wait too long for key metrics to use them effectively as productivity motivators?** This section describes a manufacturing model of this concept. With some creativity, you can apply it to a variety of settings.

The word "accountability" is used frequently. I think it means, "How do we get other people to do what they are supposed to do?" If a leader's job is to nurture others' achievement, how do we "hold" people accountable?

The manager of a central Wisconsin cranberry plant once explained to me that all employees have a goal for each day. Each day, employees decide what would make for a "perfect day"—one in which they are totally successful at reaching their targets. The plant uses a green and red light system that shows employees at a glance whether they are on track to reach their goal (green light) or not (red light). At the end of every day, management and employees briefly review what worked, what got in the way of their daily goal, what they learned, and how they would fix any problems.

Individual employee goals flow from the company goals: if there are 10,000 pounds of cranberries to move, every employee knows their individual contribution to that goal.

In healthcare, we don't have a green and red light system for ourselves or our employees to know whether we are on track with our daily goals . . . but wouldn't it be great if we did? As I listened to this plant manager talk, I wondered whether accountability lessons learned from manufacturing could be applied in a healthcare environment.

Help employees define their "perfect day." Consider implementing a 10-minute meeting with employees at the beginning of the day (or the week). Ask everyone to write down what they hope to accomplish—quick: list, go, write!

In place of green and red lights, ask people to identify where they should be halfway through the day (or week) if they remain on track (their own internal green light, clearly defined).

Establish a reputation as a manager who recaps at the end of the day or week. Ask, "Did you achieve what you set out to achieve today/this week? What got in the way if you didn't? What helped if you did? What did you learn that you can apply tomorrow?" Ask these questions in the spirit of mutual learning—we're aiming at the target together—rather than looking over someone's shoulder. Like the plant manager, sometimes we learn that employees miss their targets because of obstacles that could have been removed if we had known.

Define the "what" and "why." The plant manager told me that he does everything based on metrics—there must be a reason to do something, and it has to be measurable. How often do employees struggle to achieve because they are not clear what to do or why they are doing it? More often than we might think. Help employees see what success is by defining it, describing it, and quantifying it in whatever ways are possible. Break complex projects into chunks.

This plant manager also talked about a desire to "lift the entire community" through the work at the plant. In other words, he believes it is important to develop employees so that they spend their time away from work becoming better people (in the community in which they all live—a larger scope of accountability). Whether employees are loading cranberries, cleaning hospital rooms, or answering call lights, they know their employer is invested in them. Whether managers are getting out on the plant floor or doing what we know as "rounding," employees want to see and connect with them. They want to know that what they do matters.

Here are some easy opportunities to develop employees:

- Ask for their ideas—and listen thoughtfully.
- Use the phrase, "I could really use your help with something." Most people want to rise to the occasion.
- Ask them to help you brainstorm or problem-solve.
- Invite them to participate in community events to represent the organization.
- Delegate the fun stuff.
- Investigate their goals and support them.
- Look for and take advantage of coachable moments.
- Have them work with others on a project to learn what others do and how everyone's work is connected.
- Formalize mentoring opportunities.

At the end of the day, no one else holds us accountable. We hold ourselves accountable. A trusting work environment with clear goals and open communication clears the path.

"Few things help an individual more than to place responsibility on him, and to let him know that you trust him. . . . Every individual responds to confidence."

—Booker T. Washington

---

10. SMARTER GOALS

Are your goals boring? This isn't a trick question! The difference between a goal you might or might not achieve and the one you knock out of the park lies within you. Read this section to develop goals that will keep your daily to-do list inspired.

Most leaders know the difference between a generally stated goal, such as "I want to make things better in my department," and a SMART goal, such as "I will increase our department's employee satisfaction score from the 60th percentile to the 70th percentile in the next 12 months by implementing monthly rounding with all my employees." The second goal is SMART because it is:

- **Specific**—states what you will do
- **Measurable**—by how much
- **Attainable**—it's a stretch but within your power to achieve it
- **Relevant and Recorded**—aligned with your organizational or personal vision and written down
- **Timely**—by when

That's a good start, but there's more to it.

First: Is your heart in it? You need passion to see you through the challenges that will get in your way. When you care about your goal, you spark the continuous motivation to work on a long-term outcome. Your goal doesn't tell you the specifics of your daily to-do list. In the foregoing example, it doesn't state the detailed plan for rounding. But it does drive your decisions as you plan and conduct your rounding, prioritize your other work, and decide what to say yes or no to. Your long-term goal is your target and focus.

Dismissing the importance of the "heart" of a goal isn't good risk management. You may move forward without it, but you will be that much more distractible in a world full of ready distractions. Just ask anyone who has missed doing rounding because of schedule conflicts or a desire to avoid certain employees or situations.

How many goals are reasonable? There is no magic number, but the recommended practice is to set about five goals. Set more than five goals and it's quite possible you will achieve less, not more. There is a legendary story about Warren Buffett, the wildly successful bazillionaire, who is credited for sharing the following idea with his personal pilot:

- Write down 25 things you want to achieve in the next one to two years.
- Circle the top five. That's what you work on. You might even create one SMART goal for each of the five.
- The rest becomes your "avoid at all costs" list.

Really? Cross off a quality or customer service goal this year for the sake of employee engagement, finance, or efficiency? In healthcare, we can't ignore any of these key components, but we have to learn to manage the larger organizational picture and our work. Having too many goals will water down your focus and prevent you from achieving what matters most. Hey, if it works for Warren Buffett . . .

You have to choose. Someone I know and love set a goal very young to become a nun. Having second thoughts about giving up the chance to have her own family about a year into it, she discussed the hard decision of leaving the convent, asking, "If it doesn't work out, I could just come back, right?" A wise leader responded, "No, you must pick; then be where you are. If you are both places, you are in neither place." Having ambivalent commitment to goals, along with having too many of them, keeps us from doing our best. Goal setting is one way to do your best—not "do everything." What we choose to focus on gives us the opportunity to stretch and achieve. "Picking and sticking" also means that you don't waste energy continuing to decide (instead of moving forward toward your goals) or falling back on what seems easier.

Are they all goals? If you have more than five goals, ask yourself whether they are all goals or rather actions toward your bigger goal. Remember that strategies are your action steps toward the goal, but the goal is the end result.

Are your fates tied? Set goals with your larger team. If you can achieve your goal only if someone else fails, what does this mean for your organization's overall success and culture? Having skin in someone else's game increases accountability, breaks down "silo thinking," and keeps you focused on the bigger picture when resources are scarce.

11. WORK/LIFE . . . HOW WE BALANCE

Does it all feel like too much? There is no single solution to work-life balance, because it is different for everyone. But you know when it is too much. This section helps you build daily work habits that will prevent your tank from running empty.

Sometimes when people talk about work-life balance, the image of a teeter-totter pops up in my head:

- **Going up:** Go to work wearing armor, holding our breath and tightening our muscles to get through the day, gearing up for work to deplete our energy.
- **Going down:** Leave work, exhaling and expecting the rest of our life to help us get ready to do it all again tomorrow.

Then there is the "big" teeter-totter of a vacation, as we pin our hopes on a weeklong recharge that we hope will last for months (a tall order). We put our lives into compartments, "all or nothing," a vicious cycle on repeat. Unrelenting stress and heavy demands can lead to burnout. But consider the possibility that work can also give, not just take, our zest for life. This section offers ways to encourage ongoing rebalancing, by bringing some of that Saturday feeling to other days of the week.

Be where you are. Find joy here. Where are you right now as you read this? Look around and notice what you value. Instead of thinking, "When the weekend comes I will relax," relax now. Relax into your work. A lot of the stress we experience is a product of our expectations of how we should feel. If, in the midst of doing one thing, you find that you wish you were doing something else, or you are worrying about what comes next, you will feel unfocused and unsatisfied. That's when we start searching for balance. Instead, look for a spot of joy in the moment.

Try a balanced body posture. "I can be relaxed and focused while doing important and urgent work." Put that thought into action by changing your posture: Adopt a more relaxed pose, release your shoulders, breathe deeply, and expand your body instead of contracting it. The work is still there, but your posture in it can be engaged, interested, curious, and relaxed.

Build connection. When we laugh together, we rebalance. Bringing laughter and lightness to our work doesn't mean we are not serious about it. In what ways could you reach out to colleagues and make even small connections to foster friendship and laughter?

Make a choice. How about choosing your thoughts about work? (Note: you already *are* choosing them). When you feel stuck, remember that you can choose your thoughts, attitude, actions, moods, responses, and even how much energy you are giving to any one problem. You don't get extra credit for worrying or carrying unnecessary guilt. You may feel a surprising boost of energy when you decide to let go of that heaviness.

Plan. The old adage in project management, "When you fail to plan, you plan to fail," is true in balancing our lives, too. If you want to have a weekend away with your significant other, it won't happen if you don't make a regular time in your schedule to plan for it. If you want a report to be done on time, it won't happen if you don't carve out time on your calendar. Every area of our life benefits when we make time to reflect on our values and plan from those. You are your own scheduler. The alternative to planning is that we are just busy. Balance can be maintained if our efforts are focused and aligned, and that means planning for what matters most.

Build an uplifting work culture. Culture is everything, and leaders lead it. If employees don't have to grit their teeth and white knuckle it through a workday filled with negativity from their manager or colleagues, work can be a place they don't strive to get away from. Joy is contagious—multiple studies reinforce this (Frederickson 2009).

Remember your "why." Author Jon Gordon wrote, "We don't get burned out because of what we do; we get burned out because we forget WHY we do it" (Gordon 2017). Why do you do what you do? What parts of your work do you enjoy? Where do you get to put your unique talents to good use? Ask these questions of your team as well as yourself.

Integrate habits throughout your day. Assess your energy in real time and make resting a habit that is practiced at intervals, not just on weekends and vacations. Resting matters for our effectiveness. Imbalances can be corrected instantly when we stretch, take a short break, have a walking meeting, look up from our screen, chat with someone who makes us laugh, think about one thing to be grateful for at the top of the hour, or smile. What habits can you establish to fuel you throughout your day?

CHAPTER 4

Performance Evaluations

LEADERS INSPIRE, BUT they also manage performance. Whether you are conducting an annual review or (more importantly) an ongoing dialogue, it takes effort and intention to make sure these conversations motivate rather than deflate employees.

SELF-ASSESSMENT SCORING:

1—I am struggling with or not yet skilled at this.

2—I am starting to work on improving at this, but I need more skill building.

3—I am making some consistent progress in improving at this.

4—I am doing very well in this area.

Determine your current level of skill on these performance evaluation competencies (score 1–4):

1. I am aware of blind spots or performance issues that could derail my leadership success, and I have addressed them successfully. Score: _____

2. I have an accurate awareness of my approach to service excellence, and I go above and beyond in service to all of my customer groups. Score: _____

3. I am skilled at providing feedback, and I use specific behavioral and actionable terms so that ratings are as objective as possible. Score: _____

4. The performance evaluations I conduct show that I use both my head and my heart in a thoughtful, intentional approach to achieve positive results. Score: _____

Now explore the corresponding sections that follow to learn how to improve skills that need work or enhance your current skills.

1. SEEING OUR BLIND SPOTS

Do you wonder whether you really know your performance strengths and weaknesses? Have you had a performance review that surprised you, either positively or negatively? We tend to know our obvious strengths and weaknesses, but we all have blind spots. It's better to face your flaws and vulnerabilities. This section offers tips and resources for revealing weaknesses that we might not be able to see in ourselves.

When it is time for my own performance review, I always wonder whether I see myself accurately. One good thing about data (e.g., customer ratings, revenue generated, or number of programs delivered compared with the goal) is that it provides objective, impersonal metrics—and a good case for setting SMART goals so that you can measure whether you have achieved them. But when asked to assess myself on more subjective qualities (e.g., commitment to excellence, interpersonal influence, positive impact on culture), I have blind spots, as we all do. Maybe we get a little too puffed up about our strengths, or the opposite, we are too hard on ourselves to see the value that we bring.

Many people arrive in the manager role as a result of a series of successes. I have seen people who have experienced much success struggle the most when they fail or fall short. Unaccustomed to missing the mark, we don't always handle it well when we do. It is easy to get defensive or take feedback personally. Sometimes we are the last to know that these reactions get in our way of being perceived as an effective leader. It is in our best interest to have our blind spots revealed so that we can continue to grow. Consider the following suggestions to see yourself more clearly:

Set an intention. Before your performance review or feedback session, think of a guiding intention—a statement that will help you focus and manage your emotions should they arise. Here are some examples:

- I can learn something from all feedback.
- I will maintain an open mind.
- I choose to hear all perspectives.
- Information is just that—information.
- Q-TIP: Quit taking it personally.

Write down your guiding intention and keep it in front of you during the meeting. If you start to feel hurt or defensive during the review, look at your intention to remind yourself what is in your own best interest.

Assess yourself. Diversity of skill is a good thing; none of us can do everything well. Use the questions at the beginning of each chapter of this book for this purpose. You might even sit down with a peer to get their input as you go through the questions. Our weaknesses don't necessarily change, but we can learn to manage them better, get more mileage out of our strong suits, and keep our perspective.

Seek 360-degree feedback, even if that is not part of your organization's performance review process. Ask a mix of employees to answer a few questions about your performance. Have them sign their name, and even ask them sit down with you to share their feedback face-to-face. Some might argue that this approach does not allow employees to be anonymous and therefore more honest. But, thinking ahead, strive to create a culture in which employees can say to their manager, for example, "It is hard for me to hold people accountable for customer service behaviors such as smiling and greeting people when I see you with a frown a lot of the time." If you do offer a 360 opportunity, be rigorously nondefensive when hearing feedback. Resist the urge to explain away any negative feedback or blame others—you may do more harm than good.

Listen reflectively. Suppose your manager shares feedback like this in your performance review: "As we have discussed throughout the year, I am concerned about your follow-through on coaching your employees. Things get better for a while, but I notice them slipping back into old behaviors. When that happens, I am generally the one bringing it to your attention. I would like to see you being more proactive about this." Although you might take this feedback personally and feel bad or get defensive and try to recount all of your efforts, you can choose to pause and act differently. Reflective listening slows down defensive responses and creates a space for you to own your blind spots. Show that you are listening by replying, "It sounds like you see things improve when I coach employees on issues, but you are concerned that I am not keeping you up to date on challenges they are facing, and you would like me to bring this to you without waiting for you to ask. Is that right?" Be willing to be corrected if you haven't captured the feedback accurately. Both of you will come away with a clearer understanding.

Use thoughtful inquiry. Another response to the feedback in the last paragraph might be, "I may have some blind spots in seeing myself accurately; can you tell me more to help me understand how you came to this observation and what you would like to see instead?"

2. CAN WE ALL BE ABOVE AVERAGE?

Could you rate yourself honestly in terms of service excellence? Like blind spots, we also have biases that influence the way we view the world. When it comes to how we perform service, we tend to rate ourselves higher than may be warranted. There is always room for improvement. Read this section to see what actions you can take to be a stronger leader in this important aspect of any industry.

The opening line of Garrison Keillor's *A Prairie Home Companion* radio show about Lake Wobegon, "Where all the women are strong, all the men are good looking, and all the children are above average," is often used to describe a myth about rural life. The part about all the children being above average inspired a phenomenon known as the "Lake Wobegon effect." The term, coined by social psychologist David Myers (2015), refers to the bias we all have when we compare ourselves with others on subjective traits.

For example, when asked how we compare with others on the trait of *kindness*, we tend to think about the times we are kind, because that is more pleasant than thinking about the times we are not kind. Most people will conclude that they are kinder than the average person.

Right now you might be thinking that this effect does not apply to you. I'm sorry to tell you, that is another part of the Lake Wobegon effect. For example, we tend to think that advertising only works on *other* people, but not ourselves. If that were the case, much less money would be spent on advertising!

Think about customer service. It is good to be proud of your organization's service orientation, but it would be easy to believe you are above average. The Lake Wobegon effect suggests that if a trait matters to us, we are more likely to rate ourselves better than average on that trait. How do we *really* become above average in customer service excellence?

- **Believe that customer service is as critical as technical skill.** Because it is. When people are sick and in a hospital or clinic, they are afraid. Being technically skilled in healthcare is nonnegotiable. But technical skill can be undermined by negative interactions with even one staff member, causing customers to choose another facility next time. If you are a manager, clarify with your staff that customer service is an essential skill and hold them accountable for it. Hire for it. Reward it. Model it.

- **Everything matters.** Your behaviors, facial expressions, greetings, words, and tone of voice all send a message. In one of my own experiences as a patient, a nurse was leaving my room after registering me for a procedure. With one foot out the door, looking at her watch, she turned back to me and asked, "Oh yeah, I'm supposed to ask you if you feel safe at home." I am pretty sure that if I didn't feel safe at home, this was not the person I would have told. Does your body language say "I am here for you," "I am in your corner," "I have time for you," and "You are important?" If you are a manager, your employees are your customers, too. How would they answer these questions about your body language?

- **Develop situational awareness.** This is the opposite of scripting, which turns most people off. Be aware of what each situation calls for by *paying attention*. If your behavior standards ask you to greet customers with a smile, does enthusiastic smiling match the situation if the customer is crying or upset? One size does not fit all for communication.

- **"Delight" versus "meet expectations."** Are you delighted when you buy a new tool, bring it home, plug it in, and it works? Perhaps, if you have bought a lot of tools that don't work! But in general, we need something more to be "wowed." What is your department doing to wow the customer? Do you have ways of responding to needs that haven't been expressed yet, or to offer more than is asked for? How can you go the extra mile, fix a problem before it emerges, or beat the timeline? How do you consistently give more than is expected? With your team, identify opportunities to delight the customer.

- **Say yes when you can.** If you have to say no, think about the need the customer is trying to meet and figure out a way to meet it in another way. "Here is what I *can* do for you" feels better than "Our policy doesn't allow you to do that."

- **Recharge your enthusiasm for service on a daily basis.** When you feel like you can't give it, dig deep. Be the person who lifts others up rather than waiting for them to do it for you.

"They say motivation doesn't last. Well neither does bathing, that's why it's recommended daily."

—Zig Ziglar

---

3. THE RATINGS GAME

Do you struggle to apply performance rating scales objectively?
Unless the scale is spelled out, defining what kind of
performance earns a 10 and what earns a 1 will be a challenge.
This section offers tips on how to make performance ratings
more objective and thus meaningful and fair.

Think about an employee you consider competent and rate that
person on a 1–5 scale. Are you:

- **A tough rater?** No one gets a 5 because there is always
  room for improvement.
- **An average rater?** Yes, this person performs well, but so
  do others. No one is perfect, so let's go with a 3.
- **A high rater?** 5+++++! Exuberance!

This is the problem with rating, and one of the reasons managers
put off doing performance evaluations. Opinion-based ratings
are hard to defend, and we all exhibit rater bias. Subjective performance
rating scales are agonizing for a number of reasons:

- They offer no actionable feedback for improvement.
- When your rating differs from the employee's self-rating,
  the situation quickly becomes uncomfortable.
- Numbers mean different things to different people, leading
  to ambiguity.
- It is easy to tie one's self-esteem to a number and suffer
  needlessly from a perceived low score or fail to strive
  because of a high score.

Make rating scales useful by clarifying what the numbers mean.
Take, for example, a common target such as "teamwork." Step one:

Define terms. We all know what teamwork means, right? Maybe not. Have all your employees search for a definition of teamwork and bring it the table. Discuss the different definitions with them, find points that everyone can agree are important, and create a single definition of teamwork for your organization. Once you agree on a definition, you can move on to step two: Define the behaviors.

Behaviors are different from intentions. People may think of themselves as skillful, but the proof is in their actions—the evidence of the skill being rated. It's not hard to be specific. Think of someone who is your "poster child" for the skill you are rating and identify the behaviors that cause you to think of that person. For example, the list for teamwork might look like this:

- Consistently attends team meetings.
- Raises a hand when volunteers are needed.
- Covers for others when there is a need.
- Shows up on time and with commitments met.
- Suggests improvements that benefit the greater good, not just the individual.
- Takes actions on behalf of the team that lead to increased business or improvement.
- Is sought out by others to lead team actions.
- Is nominated for involvement in new projects because of past positive experience.
- Initiates or organizes celebration events for the team.
- Recognizes others on the team for their contributions so that they feel appreciated.
- Speaks up respectfully when conflict emerges to encourage resolution.
- Avoids speaking about other team members behind their backs.
- Suggests team decision-making approaches that fit the situation (consensus, majority vote, leader decision, etc.).

The third step: Decide how to assign rankings. To make it simple, someone who consistently exhibits all of these qualities is a high performer, a 5. Those who demonstrate none or few of these behaviors are low performers, the 1s or 2s. Those who rate as 3s show about half of these qualities, while 4s demonstrate more than half and do so more consistently than 3s. This process doesn't remove all subjectivity, but it will make your dialogue in coaching and performance evaluation discussions—sharing specific examples of times when you did or did not see the behaviors—much more conducive to improvement going forward.

4. LEADING WITH HEART AND HEAD WHEN EVALUATING

Do performance reviews keep you up at night? Join the club. Many of us struggle to get performance evaluations right. A key part of that is recognizing the importance of building relationships of trust with your employees. Evaluating requires both head and heart. This section offers ideas for how to do that and how to manage yourself in the process.

A participant in one of my performance evaluation workshops encouraged his fellow leaders to be courageous in giving "hard to deliver" news. He openly shared his experience of hearing a tough message about his own performance a decade earlier. Because his manager had shared his concerns openly and honestly, this leader was inspired to go back to school and to work on his self-development. He admitted that the feedback was tough to hear, but as a result, he achieved things he might never have done if his manager had worried about hurting his feelings and held back from giving him honest feedback.

I know many managers lay awake at night and worry about giving constructive feedback. They are concerned that the recipient will be hurt, defensive, or angry. As a leader, it helps to find a way to transform that worrying (an energy waster) into a "leading with heart" statement: "I want you to be successful, so I will be honest when I see you doing things that get in your way or when I have ideas that can help you grow."

Here are a few ideas that might help you make this transformation:

- **Be intentional.** Specifically, make a choice that you are entering into these coaching or review sessions with the *purpose* of your employee's success. Tell your employees that your intention is to help them be their best— something you both want.

- **Remember that tears are not fatal.** Worrying that someone will cry is no reason to hold back information that ultimately will help them. When you approach employees in a caring and honest way, you can't guarantee that it won't hurt a little. But we grow when we feel that tension, not when we are completely comfortable.

- **Work only as hard as your employees work on their success.** I learned this from a therapist I once supervised who said that he only worked as hard as his clients did on their problems. If they gave it 100 percent, so did he. If they gave it 50 percent, so did he. When your heart is in it more than theirs is, you are left feeling frustrated and resentful. At the end of the day, we are responsible for making something of our life—no one can do it for us.

- **Think of giving feedback as holding up a mirror.** For example, imagine that you need to tell an employee that their habit of heavy sighing and mumbling under their breath while they work is affecting the team. Say what you see (the sighing and mumbling) rather than stating what you think is the reason (that the employee is negative or has a bad attitude—both of which are subjective judgments). Judgments can be argued, so stick to specific behaviors. Sometimes people are unaware of their own behaviors. At other times, they are aware of their behaviors, but they don't realize the impact they have on others.

- **It's OK to be tenderhearted.** That doesn't mean you can't become skilled at giving constructive feedback. It shouldn't ever be so easy to deliver tough news that we don't stop to consider how the recipient will feel hearing it. Leading with the heart means that sometimes your heart may feel heavy, but that is not a permanent condition (thank goodness). It also means that you might want to . . .

- **Practice your delivery of difficult feedback with a mentor or your manager.** It is likely that your colleagues have dealt with similar situations in the past. Support each other in holding these conversations so that you can build confidence and skill.

CHAPTER 5

Teaching and Facilitating

As a leader, at some point you will have to put yourself in front of others and get your point across. You will have to manage a crowd, teach people, or help a group understand something better. The skills covered in this chapter will help you connect with an audience more effectively.

SELF-ASSESSMENT SCORING:

1—I am struggling with or not yet skilled at this.

2—I am starting to work on improving at this, but I need more skill building.

3—I am making some consistent progress in improving at this.

4—I am doing very well in this area.

Determine your current level of skill on these facilitation competencies (score 1–4):

1. I can get a group of people to actively participate in a discussion when I ask for input. Score: _____

2. My communication in a virtual environment (e.g., presenting a webinar) is engaging and powerful. Score: _____

3. I make effective use of meaningful stories and examples in my speaking to convey my message. Score: _____

4. I can succinctly summarize a project or situation in a meaningful but brief overview. Score: _____

Now explore the corresponding sections that follow to learn how to improve skills that need work or enhance your current skills.

1. HEARING CRICKETS

Have you ever asked for feedback or questions from a group and gotten the sound of silence? You may have hoped for a lot of interaction, but no one speaks up. This section offers simple ideas for encouraging meaningful audience participation.

Crickets are what you dread hearing when you ask people for their input or ideas during a staff meeting. It is one of the reasons some leaders stop asking for input—it is uncomfortable and discouraging to be met with silence. You want your staff to be as engaged as you are, but when they don't speak up, it can seem like they are not. Don't give up. Simple facilitation techniques can help draw people out.

First, clarify your question. All skilled facilitation starts here. What do you *really* want to know? Consider the difference between these two examples:

- Version 1: "Are you getting through your performance evaluations with staff?" A simple head nod or shake will do. Asking the question in this way implies that it is OK if the answer is no. If you are asking because you have a concern, consider instead . . .

- Version 2: "What barriers are you running into in completing performance reviews with your staff by the due date?" Asking about barriers shows that you are willing to help remove those barriers and make your priorities clear. Thoughtful, open-ended questions provide an opportunity to reinforce your expectations and avoid yes/no responses.

Encourage partner discussions. This is my go-to practice. In a large group, people may think, "Someone else will answer. I don't need to stick my neck out." When asked to talk with a partner, though, there is no escaping participation. You can mix up the discussion by asking people to talk with someone who is not sitting next to them. Simply count off, draw a number out of a bag, or put letters on each seat prior to match up staff members before starting the meeting. For example, if you are concerned that your question might be met with crickets, ask people to discuss it with a partner for a few minutes. Then regroup and ask about the issues that came up in their partner discussions.

Wait. If you ask, it helps to give people a minute to think. Take a drink of water, write down a note, and take a couple of breaths. Someone will talk.

Use flip charts. Again using mixed groups, ask staff to go use flip charts and brainstorm ideas or answers to the question or problem you are trying to solve. If you want different people to speak up besides the usual suspects, assign a spokesperson for each group. For example, "The spokesperson for each group will be the person who has the longest commute to work."

Brainstorm with sticky notes. Give everyone a stack of sticky notes and a pen. Pose your question or problem. Ask everyone to write down their ideas or solutions, one per note. After a few minutes, ask the participants to post all of their ideas on the wall, then have small groups organize the notes into themes. It can be effective to begin this sorting process silently. Once everyone has had a chance to participate, discuss what the themes reveal. This is a simple affinity process that allows people to see a problem and its solutions differently. It may reveal an emerging consensus.

Don't talk—write. Not everyone gets out of first gear by talking. Pose your question or issue and ask people to take a few minutes to write down their thoughts. They won't have to show it to anyone, but the time spent thinking and writing gives them fuel to start the discussion.

Pass the paper. Ask each person to write down a clear challenge or problem. Then, everyone passes their paper to the right and then writes down *any* idea that comes to mind for about a minute. Repeat this process a few times. Fresh eyes, and sometimes even unconventional ideas, can spark discussion and may generate new solutions.

Have a "go-around." Follow up a question by asking the group, "Let's go around the table and everyone share one reaction, idea, your current status." Allow people to pass, but keep in mind that frequent passing signals an individual coaching opportunity with that employee.

2. DISTANCE LEARNING TIPS

When you are presenting virtually, do you ever feel as if you are talking to yourself? This section offers ideas from a non-"techie" to make webinars less painful and more effective.

I'm an old-school teacher: When I teach a workshop, I want to do it in person. I still believe that in-person learning and dialogue are best—and for some things, it is. But the COVID-19 pandemic has changed the way we organize meetings and classrooms, perhaps forever. Out of necessity, we are adapting to make distance learning work. I've made a lot of mistakes in embracing this technology. This section offers the top ten things I have learned the hard way—some of which I even picked up from a very effective webinar (yes, I learned in a webinar!) on this very topic (Machovina 2014).

- **Smile, you're on camera.** Just like talking into a microphone, for most people, being on camera pushes us out of our comfort zone. We'd rather just show our slides. Facial interaction makes a huge difference, though, as it comes closer to the experience of being in the same room as your audience. Use your camera so that people can see you.
- **Make eye contact with the camera as if it were a person.** Look at the camera, not the screen off to the side or down toward your desk. Set up your space so that the notes or screen you are looking at are not angled away from the camera. This can be challenging to do, but when you look somewhere other than the camera, it is like talking to someone without making eye contact.
- **Have more than one voice.** Share the presenting with another person (or people) to break up the vocal tones for the listener.
- **Ask participants to write on your slides.** Use the tools that are available to you. If you don't know how to use them, spend some time experimenting. Explore whether the platform you are using includes annotation tools which allow participants to type onto the screen in real time to vote or answer a question. Polls work, too, but they take advance coordination, whereas annotation can be used spontaneously. Sometimes, polls are used to break up content but don't have any real value for the learner. When using polls, consider whether the results will actually be of interest to the audience.

- **Keep it short and focused.** Keep your presentation to 45 minutes or less and one to three key points. If you are merely talking at people and throwing a lot of content at them, in most cases, your purpose will not be served. It's like the old adage, "Telling is not teaching."
- **Have helpers.** Ask a colleague to manage the equipment, track the chat, monitor questions, and deal with technical difficulties so that you aren't distracted by them.
- **Teach the technology before the webinar begins.** Offer participants the option to sign on 15 minutes early if they don't know how to use the platform's features. If you spend your meeting time doing this, participants who are already familiar with the technology may tune out.
- **Use some kind of annotation every ten minutes.** Participants will be tempted to check their email or text messages during the webinar. It is human nature to believe, mistakenly, that we can multi-task. Create opportunities to reengage them frequently by asking a question that requires a response.
- **Speak personably.** Look into the camera and visualize the lens as your audience. Simply reading your presentation from a script is a sure way to lose your audience.
- **Give clear instructions if you are using offline small-group discussions.** During in-person trainings, it is easy to answer questions and remind groups what they are discussing. When meeting in person, you can fill in the gaps. When the discussion goes offline, that disconnection is an invitation to check out.

Bonus tip: Ask participants to come prepared with sticky notes, pen, paper, advance assignments, flip charts, and markers. Just like an in-person meeting, you want the participants to have tools to work with. It's hard to hold a marker and send text messages at the same time.

Simply replacing in-person methods of facilitation and teaching with a computer screen has left many of us turned off to the whole idea. We have to adapt with fresh approaches.

3. STORY TIME

> **Have you heard other speakers make effective use of stories and examples and wish you had that skill?** You do have it. You have your own stories. This section shows you how to turn your experiences into ready stories that will help make your messages stick.

John Medina, the author of *Brain Rules* (2008), argues that emotions are what gets the brain's attention. We need meaning before we can understand details. When you are telling a story, the listener wants to understand why it matters much more than "First this happened, then that happened . . ." A brief, well-placed, and relevant story enhances learning by hooking into the listener's emotions. We remember the lessons from stories because of this emotional connection.

Stories have an important place in a leader's coaching and teaching. Spend a little time recalling and writing down experiences that seem worth sharing. You can use them effectively in moments when they matter.

To get started, collect your most significant milestones:

Failures. Unpleasant as they are, failures are great teachers. Consider these questions: What did failure teach you about yourself? What did you remember going forward? How did you forgive yourself and move on? What did failure teach you about the value of humility, asking for help, saying no, and knowing your strengths and weaknesses? Are there any phrases you have incorporated into your daily thinking to prevent repeating a mistake? **Use for:** normalizing the fact that we all fail sometimes; it is what we do with failure that matters.

Success against the odds. These are the times when you didn't think you could do it, but you did. How did you keep from quitting when it seemed impossible? Where did you seek support and resources? What pushed you outside your comfort zone, and why was it worth it? **Use for:** encouraging someone to grow or reminding someone that we can't reach the goals we don't try for. It is especially helpful for those who look up to you or believe they could never do what you do. You can also use these stories to build commitment to change initiatives.

Turning points. Recall some of the critical junctures in your life: the experiences that have made you who you are but wouldn't appear on your résumé. Think back to your childhood for key moments that stand out: "This is one thing that made me the person I am today." What tough decisions have you made that changed the course of your life? What moves were difficult, courageous, or bold *for you*, without which you would not have had subsequent successes and joys? What doors opened because you did the hard thing? **Use for:** helping someone who is at a turning point and reminding them of the strengths built from their own significant life events.

Aha! moments. Recall moments when you thought, "I finally get it!" For example, a micromanager who learned to trust his employees when he realized how he was getting in their way. How did an aha moment open your eyes? What was the benefit? **Use for:** nudging the listener to consider the other side of a problem or coaching someone with limited self-awareness.

Funny moments. Life is better when we laugh a little, especially at ourselves. When have you *decided* to see the humor in your experience, and how did that change your mindset? **Use for:** helping someone gain perspective when they are beating themselves up.

Here are some general tips for using stories in your teaching and speaking:

- When teaching, have one story ready for each major learning objective. You may not use all the stories, but thinking about them in advance will prepare you for in-the-moment delivery.
- Share the stage. Eliciting others' stories can be powerful, too. Be ready, though, to manage others who share too often, go on too long, or veer off topic.
- When coaching, sharing stories in every session might backfire on you. Balance sharing with inquiry to help people discover their own stories. For example, "Have you ever faced a similar challenge? How did you work through it? What did you learn?"
- Keep your stories fresh. Old stories are great and often worth retelling, but *you* will get bored by them, and it will show.

Sometimes, however, you may want to skip the story. For example, leave out the story in these situations:

- When you need to tell it more than the listener needs to hear it. Though you own the story, you must ask yourself why you are telling it.
- When people start to fidget. This can be hard to read, but overuse of storytelling diminishes your influence and frustrates the audience. Think "judicious" use. Ask someone you trust to give you feedback after a presentation or staff meeting to gauge whether your stories

hit or missed the mark, were too brief or too long, or were too frequent or sparse.

- When confidentiality could be breached. Your story may be relatable for an employee, but in telling it, you could inadvertently identify who you are talking about. Only tell the story if you can credibly adapt it to protect everyone's privacy.

4. SUMMARIZING

When someone asks you for a summary, do you find it difficult to sort through the multitude of details? Do you include too much information or, alternatively, share so little that you miss the key points? Summarizing helps people understand when it provides just enough information. Creating clear, useful summaries is a skill you can develop. This section offers some exercises to practice and specific methods for getting it right.

"A picture is worth a thousand words" could be the motto for the skill of summarizing. Less is more. Imagine that you have just participated in a lengthy project meeting, and your manager asks for a summary of what transpired. It is not easy to do this well. What do you leave in? What details do you weed out? The devil may be in the details, but the details do not belong in a summary. Sorting, discerning, and zeroing in on the broad message are skills that you can strengthen. Doing so will bolster your ability to influence others.

Practice summarizing the following example:

Your project meeting covered overtime work on a project that is over budget, maternity leaves in a particular department resulting in staff shortages, unrealistic timelines causing delays, and difficulty scheduling meetings because of time constraints. The meetings are scheduled by the project manager based on her schedule, and attendance has been hit or miss for attendance because people have other commitments. The meeting minutes are lengthy and come out right before the next meeting, so they are of little use. The team came up with a plan for establishing agreed-upon limits on overtime, revised the project timeline to accommodate leave, and set regular recurring meeting dates to improve attendance. Several ideas were shared for improving the meeting minutes for people who could not attend, including using the agenda as a guide to meeting notes (with agenda items rewritten as SMART goals) and noting only decisions made instead of "discussion" items, which went on and on and which people did not read. Decisions were made on revisions to the budget and how to adapt the original plan to meet the goals without additional funds. This will be done by first identifying and then eliminating some costs that are not value added. The roles and responsibilities worksheet was updated to identify who will take action on each action item with timelines added to keep people on track. This worksheet also helped confirm that everyone had a piece of the work and was taking ownership.

- **Start with the punchline.** Unlike jokes, put your ending statement first. Meaning is found in the bottom line. Without including any of the details about the content that was discussed, write one sentence that conveys the essence of the meeting.

- **Look for themes.** If you put all the meeting details onto separate notes and then scanned them and sorted them into piles with commonalities, what headings would you use? These headings reveal your themes.

- **Apply the "rule of three."** Limiting yourself to three themes can prevent you from getting too granular, and it is a good number for your listener to grab onto. Any one of the three themes opens up opportunities for more detailed discussion *if requested*—but remember, you are giving a summary, not a detailed report. List the details of the project example on separate sticky notes and sort them into three piles. Then, create a heading for each one, and you'll have your three themes.

- **Raise your lens.** The project in the example is fairly straightforward. When a discussion is more complex and doesn't easily lend itself to themes, start instead with a higher-level adjective. *Robust, divergent, enlightening, enthusiastic,* and *painful* are words that set the big-picture tone for the listener. Think of a discussion that you have taken part in and pick an adjective to describe it. Follow with . . .

- **Compare and contrast.** With a big body of work, summarize by showcasing breadth. Add to your adjective a phrase showcasing the extremes of the discussion. Example: "The heated discussion on this project covered the gamut of ditching the project altogether all the way to some members digging in their heels to keep it on life support, and everything in between, ending with no firm decision."

- **Practice.** At your next meeting (or workshop you attend, book you read, or discussion you have), practice summarizing with a partner and ask for feedback. Come up with the punchline, themes, adjectives, and compare and contrast to describe the breadth of the discussion. Try to state these in 90 seconds.

CHAPTER 6

Self-Awareness

SELF-AWARENESS MUST PRECEDE self-management. For that reason, self-awareness is fundamental to your success. Self-awareness is like looking in the mirror long enough to know yourself but not gazing so long that you become self-absorbed. Becoming and staying aware takes intentional practice. This chapter examines the concept of self-awareness from a variety of angles and offers suggestions for developing your self-awareness.

SELF-ASSESSMENT SCORING:

1—I am struggling with or not yet skilled at this.

2—I am starting to work on improving at this, but I need more skill building.

3—I am making some consistent progress in improving at this.

4—I am doing very well in this area.

Determine your current level of skill on these self-awareness competencies (score 1–4):

1. I don't let powerful people intimidate me, nor do I deny that I may be intimidating to others, even if I don't see myself that way. Score: _____

2. I understand the difference between ego and self-confidence. I know when my ego is taking over my thinking, and I have strategies to keep my ego in check. Score: _____

3. I am patient even in frustrating situations. Score: _____

4. I take rejuvenating breaks regularly. Score: _____

5. I accept that I cannot make everyone like me or my decisions as a leader. I nurture trusting relationships without taking it personally if someone doesn't like me. Score: _____

6. I manage myself kindly when I fail, and I look for the lessons and opportunities when things don't go as planned. Score: _____

7. I regularly review my work to make sure that the goals my team is pursuing have value. I can make the hard decision to end a project, even if it is a favorite of mine, because it no longer supports my organization's priorities. Score: _____

8. I effectively manage my fears and anxieties about _____ (e.g., the future, making a mistake, admitting that I don't know everything, etc.). Score: _____

9. I know when to resist the urge to offer to help too quickly and allow others to struggle so that they can grow. Score: _____

10. I don't get defensive when I hear tough feedback on my performance. I can find something to learn from in all feedback. Score: _____

11.   I am willing to accept the awkwardness of learning something new as a necessary part of building competence. Score: _____

12.   Guilt does not consume my energy. Score: _____

Now explore the corresponding sections that follow to learn how to improve skills that need work or enhance your current skills.

1. INTIMIDATION

> **Is there someone who intimidates you? Or, has someone hinted that you might be intimidating to others?** Simply holding a leadership role increases the odds that some people will find you intimidating. Read this section to explore your beliefs about intimidation and to understand how you can be more approachable and willing to approach others.

"No one can make you feel inferior without your consent."
—Eleanor Roosevelt

I would add a friendly amendment to Eleanor Roosevelt's wise quotation: Intimidation generally requires our consent as well. Think of people who have intimidated you in the past but no longer have that hold on you. Who changed? Likely the change occurred in your own mind. Intimidation is connected to fear, and our fears are created by our thoughts. We can change how we think. The following are seeds that foster intimidation:

- **Role ambiguity.** Knowing what is expected of us increases our chances of success. I asked my husband, a veteran, whether his army officers were intimidating.

Surprisingly (to me), he said, "No, not really. You knew the rules, and it was clear what would get you into—or keep you out of—trouble." If ambiguity in your work environment causes you to feel intimidated, consider asking for clarity, stating your purpose, and asking for your needs to be met. For example, "I want to be successful and do my best, but I need your help to understand what is expected of me."

- **Threat of loss.** You may be intimidated by a person who has the power to fire you or take away something you value, such as freedom or autonomy. How does this threat impact your work? Do you automatically make that person's request a top priority? Doing so can create problems when more important work gets pushed aside. Even if you do get all of your work done, you create stress for yourself. Examine your beliefs with a reality check: Would you really get fired if you treated the intimidating person the same way you treat others? Are you assuming too much? What would happen if you explained how the person's request ranks among your other priorities, rather than merely accepting the person's demands? Alternatively, what if you shared the multiple priorities you are juggling and ask the person to help you order them?

- **Fear of exposure.** It is not only people in positions of authority who can be intimidating. If you are intimidated by one of your employees, you might fear that they know your weakness and will use it against you. Neglecting to hold employees accountable for their weak spots gives them an unhealthy power in the organization. The perception that you are playing favorites weakens morale. Are there mistakes that you need to own up to and fix? If that's the case, do so and move on. Prepare for your coaching session with the intimidating employee to avoid getting derailed into a conversation about your mistakes.

Assume that *you are intimidating* to someone else, too. When you move into a leadership role, understand that others' perceptions of you will shift. Promotion creates a power differential that cannot be denied. Use the power you have with great care.

You can better understand how others perceive you by asking who in your workplace would agree—or, more importantly, disagree—with these statements:

- I am easy to talk to and approach.
- I am open and willing when asked for help.
- I am a pleasure to work with.
- My body language conveys genuine interest and respect for all.
- I always greet others in a friendly way.
- Reflective listening is natural for me.
- When I am given tough feedback, I accept it graciously without defensiveness.

2. EGO

Can you recognize when your ego takes over and makes things worse for you? This critical self-awareness skill will save you a great deal of angst and remove a lot of fear for your team. This section helps you explore what it looks and sounds like when you have lost your perspective. It offers techniques for putting your ego in its place.

From Donald Trump to the Dalai Lama, ego is a force that we all must face—not just once but many times a day on most days. Even the most enlightened of us battle with our ego from time to time. Most of us would not want to be described as arrogant, self-absorbed, or egomaniacal. But it is difficult feedback to hear about yourself or to give it to someone else.

Your ego might be rearing its ugly head if you find yourself doing these things:

- Feeling irritated by or jealous of a colleague's success
- Mentally or verbally downplaying another's talents
- Seeking recognition
- Not listening because you are waiting to interrupt
- Deciding that you are right and another person is wrong before you know the whole situation
- Stewing over your mistakes
- Believing that the people around you are dimwits
- Making self-deprecating comments that you know are insincere
- Getting defensive when others give you feedback

Do you see yourself in these statements? Most likely, we all can connect with at least one item in this list. To lead with integrity, for the good of all, we must learn to leave our ego at the door. But how do we throw out the uninvited guest called ego?

Don't confuse ego with self-confidence. Many leaders shy away from owning their self-confidence because they fear looking egotistical. Self-confidence is about *authentically* accepting your strengths and weaknesses, not spinning a story about either. Self-confidence is not threatened by others' success or ideas unlike your own. Longing for outside recognition or feeling envious may be signs that you need to acknowledge your strengths. Build self-confidence by taking an honest inventory of your strengths and not-so-strong suits. Everyone has both. Look at yourself with a scientist's mind (facts and data), not a judgmental mind (I'm good or bad). Pay attention to those you see as confident but not egomaniacal and observe how they exhibit confidence in their behaviors.

Establish credit. Who do you need to thank today? Someone contributed something to whatever you are doing successfully. Make a daily habit of humbly reflecting on who inspired, taught, encouraged, supported, or nudged you. Find a way to pass on the credit.

Consider alternatives. A decisive communication style works in many situations, but it can backfire when it is not applied with care. As a leader, your decisiveness may close the door to others' ideas or engagement. Once you make up your mind about something, consider at least two alternatives. Ask your team to improve your idea in at least two ways.

Transform your anger before coaching. If you are angry when someone doesn't perform to your standards, that anger is a sign that you are taking matters personally—ego! Let go of your anger and reframe the situation by considering how you can help that person develop. The behavior of others is not about you. That doesn't mean you must lower your standards. It means you must communicate your standards and expectations clearly and objectively through constructive dialogue. Coaching is about helping people grow, not putting them in their place.

Work on accepting your mistakes. Humility in the face of mistakes is one thing that makes a leader accessible and real to people. Ego, on the other hand, bristles at mistakes, hides them, or broods in a pot of self-absorption (I know this one too well). My strategy is to tell myself, "Get over yourself." Another strategy is to imagine how you would treat a colleague who made the same mistake and treat yourself with the same compassion.

Give five. For five minutes each day, help someone with a task or goal that benefits them, not you—and don't tell anyone about it. Pay attention to how helping another person makes you feel about yourself. This technique helps us get out of our own head, where ego resides.

Volunteer for a project in which you do not have expertise. This strategy is about staying humble and curious. Keep learning, seeking, and challenging what you believe and what you know. Ego is more comfortable "knowing for sure." Self-confidence means being open to new ideas, being willing to learn, and accepting that you will be wrong sometimes.

3. PRACTICING PATIENCE

Are you impatient? Then read this section. It won't cure you, but it may give you a new perspective and ideas for developing patience.

I am that person who repeatedly hits the elevator button when the door doesn't open immediately. I click web links multiple times when they fail to open right away. As I was standing in a grocery checkout line thinking about this topic, I found myself getting steamed at the person ahead of me who was slowly counting out exact change. (I'm happy to report that I caught myself quickly and had a good laugh at my own expense.)

We tell people that impatience is a personality trait, and it feels like a part of our identity that is hardwired. Saying "I have *no* patience" makes it sound as if patience is something I could have but choose not to—and that is accurate. Impatience is a choice and a behavior; therefore, we can choose to behave differently if we want to.

Why should a leader think about becoming more patient?

- **For your health.** The cost of impatience accrues mostly to the impatient. The upshot of three reports on the impact of impatience from the *Journal of Biosocial Science*, the *Journal of the American Medical Association*, and *Science Daily* was summed up in a National Public Radio story as "Impatience makes us tense, fat and broke" (Weeks 2010).

- **For your employees.** We want the best performance from employees. We can get compliance ("I'll do it") when we pressure others, but can we get engagement ("I'll do it with commitment, excellence, and passion")? Do you motivate using nudges? ("I believe you can do this, you can dig a little deeper; I'm in your corner.") Or does it feel more like impatience to employees? ("I've got my doubts about you; you might not be fast enough or good enough.")

Would you like to work at lengthening your fuse?

Be an actor. Put yourself in situations you know will make you impatient and *act* like a patient person. "Fake it 'til you make it" is a common saying for good reason. Find the longest line at the grocery store and wait in it. While you are waiting, focus on breathing calmly, making a mental list of people who helped you that day, whose lives you had an impact on that day, or something good about each of your employees.

Tell yourself a different story. The actions we display when we are impatient (sighing, fidgeting, getting red in the face, feeling irritated, holding our breath) are not necessarily automatic. Just as in conflict situations, impatient behaviors originate in the stories we tell ourselves. "Don't these people know what they are doing? This computer is a piece of &^:+$#@! Nothing ever works out for me!" Question the stories you tell yourself and create alternatives to change your perspective.

Decide what matters most *right now*. Is it most important to get the work done fast or your way, or is there greater value in gaining your employee's trust? Sometimes being the quickest does matter most. But if that is always your demeanor, employees will feel only pressure rather than support.

Does your behavior serve you? Once you decide what matters most, consider whether your actions match that priority. At any given moment, ask yourself whether what you are thinking or doing is serving you and your employees to achieve what matters most.

Patience does not mean passivity. Being more patient doesn't mean lowering your standards, giving someone 1,000 chances, or forgoing deadlines. It's about the "how" rather than the "what" of the work that we do and that we ask others to do. Sometimes our impatience with another person indicates we have not been as clear or direct as we need to be. In an effort to appear patient, we may have communicated with less urgency and inadvertently left the person in the dark as to our real needs.

Be patient with yourself. Or not. Impatience is not *all* negative, but if you are feeling ill effects from it—or if others are—it may be time to ask whether the personal costs of your impatience outweigh the benefits and make a course correction.

4. HIT PAUSE: TAKING A BREAK WHEN YOU DON'T THINK YOU HAVE TIME

Do you believe you don't have time to take a break? In reality, you don't have time *not* to. This section helps you become more aware of the barriers you put in your own way and the benefits to taking them down. It offers a couple of simple measures that you can take throughout the day to rejuvenate yourself.

In weightlifting, it's generally recommended that you do as many reps—with care and control—as possible, until you can do no more. If you can do endless reps without fatigue, your weights may be too light, and you likely won't see the same results. If you can only do a couple of reps, your weights are probably too heavy, and you risk injury. The sweet spot is somewhere in the middle.

The goal is to break down the muscle, rest to allow the muscle to rebuild and grow stronger, then go at it again.

Research on highly successful athletes reveals a key strategy for success following this very pattern: Push yourself as far as you can, then recover (Loehr and Schwartz 2003). If we applied this strategy to our work, we would work hard, give it our all, and take breaks periodically. But we're not very good at the "take breaks" part.

The same science tells us that even *pausing* for a few moments throughout the day can make us more productive, creative, innovative, and alert. So why don't we do it?

- We feel guilty because no one else is taking breaks.
- It feels like we are wasting time.
- We believe we get more done when we work longer and continue to push ourselves.
- We are afraid that others will think we are lazy or goofing off.
- We believe others expect us to keep working.
- We are afraid if we stop, we'll never start again!

For optimal results, we need both the stress of expending energy and rest to recover it. When we have too much of either, we get the same results as a weightlifter. Too much expenditure results in injury (mistakes, rework, spinning, irritability, less productivity with longer hours). Too much rest causes us to go slack (bored, restless, unmotivated).

Take a few minutes to rebalance. Try these ideas:

- **Set an alarm every hour to take a one-minute stretch break.** You may think it feels silly, but research on productivity tells us otherwise (Bregman 2011).
- **Get out of your chair hourly if you have a desk job.** Go outside and take a couple of deep breaths. Nature is restorative and refuels us, even if we are not in the woods.

- **Do an hourly body scan.** Take one minute at the top of the hour and check in with your body: Are you hunching forward in your chair, slumping, frowning, clenching your jaw or your fists, holding your breath, or holding tension in any part of your body? For one minute, release that tension. Being aware of it and letting it go for a minute is a break. (It's not like a week in the Caribbean, but it does restore energy.)

- **Be a friend.** Want engaged employees? People with good friends at work are more likely to be engaged, which means higher productivity and more results (Mann 2018). When I see my colleagues Lauri and Kim walk by a couple times a day to get coffee together, I smile because I know their friendship and a few minutes talking about something other than work energizes them when they return to their cubicles. They get more accomplished by taking a short break than if they spent those minutes staying on task at their desks.

- **Keep a glass of water close by and drink it.** Water replenishes energy and helps us burns calories. Often when we feel tired or hungry, we really are thirsty. (I know what you are thinking: If I drink water, I'll have to take a bathroom break, and I don't have time for that. Yes, you do!)

5. THE NEED TO BE LIKED

Does the desire to be liked prevent you from doing or saying things that need to be done or said? Alternatively, do you give little or no thought to whether people like you? This section offers perspectives on these two positions, both of which can make you less effective as a leader.

A former college president quoted James Schorr, a marketing executive for Holiday Inns, Inc., when asked about her provocative leadership style: "Some of the most talented people are terrible leaders because they have a crippling need to be loved by everyone."

This college president talked about how this statement describes most of us. We all want to be liked, but to be a leader, you have to be able to withstand discord (Ziff 2010). Some people are not going to like you if you are a successful leader. Or, perhaps more accurately, the fear of not being liked will keep some people from becoming great leaders.

Few people would say that they *prefer* being disliked. But when does the need for approval get in the way of being an effective leader or manager? Holding back honest feedback from employees because you fear they won't like you means that you are not doing your job.

It's like a nurse who would say to a patient, "Oh, the IV hurts? Ok then, I won't give you this lifesaving medicine because I don't want to hurt you." We know that even if a medical procedure causes pain, we have to do it to help the patient in the long run. How you do it makes a big difference to the patient's response. A nurse who can explain, reassure, listen, empathize with, and encourage the patient will get much higher marks in patient satisfaction than one who tells the patient to "suck it up."

When employees are having performance issues—either technical or behavioral—and you don't address them because you are afraid they won't like you, you are keeping their "medicine" from them, and it *hurts* them.

How and why you give feedback makes a difference. Marcus Buckingham, in his book *The One Thing You Need to Know . . . About Great Managing, Great Leading and Sustained Individual Success* (2005, 81), emphasizes the need to care about your employees and to relate to them as people:

> [This does not imply] that good managers are soft on their
> people. On the contrary, good managers are willing to deal

quickly with poorly performing employees precisely because they want each employee to succeed, and, on a visceral level, they cannot stand the sight of someone they care about staggering along at a mediocre level of performance. Counterintuitive though it may sound, the caring manager confronts poor performance early.

Here is some food for thought:

- How do you want to be remembered by your employees when *they* retire?
- Think about feedback *you* have received that may have been hard to hear. How did it help you grow?
- Examine your need to be liked. What would happen if you weren't?
- Consider that it may also be problematic if you are not concerned at all about whether employees like you.
- Think about how it would feel to be respected but not necessarily "loved" by your employees.
- Create a support network for yourself among your peers. They are dealing with the same challenges you are. You can encourage each other to do the difficult things—like "management IVs."

6. EPIC FAIL

Do you fear failure? While most people don't like it, failure is not all bad. This section offers a viewpoint on blame and suggestions for reframing failure.

In healthcare, to pursue relentless quality, it is critical to be constantly on the lookout for failure, to the point of preoccupation. This is not easy for those who are promoted for doing well.

Many try to *avoid* failure because they find it uncomfortable; it is even worse for those who are perfectionists. The statement "It's OK to make mistakes" can be interpreted as "It is OK for *you* to make mistakes, but not for me." This is a deep-seated belief, and it might be time to unseat it. Failure is a gift. Look back. What failures have you learned the most from?

It is understandable that we may be "failures" at managing failure. It is natural to prefer success, and we grow up getting rewarded for it. No one wants to get in trouble for an error; we have all seen someone who has paid a high price for one. We see constant examples of leaders who regularly turn to blame instead of modeling accountability and learning from mistakes. At every turn, we find this blaming tactic:

- **In our world.** Every day, news headlines prompt us to assign blame. As a culture, we want to find someone to blame for failure. We look to spin a story, make excuses, or blame others—tactics that are hardwired early in life to avoid disappointing others or getting punished. Start to read news stories with a critical eye for blame. Search for the facts, taking judgment out of the equation.

- **In our organization.** This hardwiring is evident in our workplace environment as well. If missteps reveal a culture of blame, start a conversation about transitioning to a culture of learning. Establish an organizational "ground rule" to tell the truth and then make it safe to do so. Think of leaders who admit their mistakes and work to make things right. This is authentic, human leadership, and these are the people we want to follow.

- **In our teams.** It can be frustrating to address a problem with someone who refuses to see their own part in that problem. Address "He started it" with, "What are you doing to keep it going?" Meet "It's her fault" with, "What part do you own?" Many who err are looking for someone to say, "It's OK," or eventually it will be. Hone your leadership muscle by learning to say that to yourself. If you are already programmed to talk to yourself this way, help others move toward this self-reassurance.

- **In ourselves.** Do you tend to react to your mistakes by looking for someone to blame? The next time you discover a mistake, stop and pay attention to your thought process. Learn to recognize when you are blaming and decide instead to review your own actions objectively. As you speak about the failure, reflect on what you know to be true—just the facts, presented without emotion.

As you reflect on the blaming habits that you see around you and within you, use the following strategies to become more at ease with accepting—and making good use of—the discomfort that comes when you miss the mark.

- **Nurture a friendship with someone who will help put your failures in perspective.** Friends or mentors can help you to focus on what can be learned from a failure and rebalance when you are thrown off. Ask them to call you out when you act defeated or defensive—signs that you are being over- or under-accountable.

- **Fail on purpose.** Try something you are pretty sure will not work (not with a patient, though!), with the intention of keeping your mind open to learning. Do something you know you will succeed at to remind you that some things *do* work out. Use this experiment to reinforce that neither success nor failure is a permanent condition.

Healthcare patients who have suffered from our failures most often say that *they just don't want it to happen to someone else.* Transparency means that we talk about and own what went wrong and prevent its reoccurrence. Be the leader who creates the kind of environment in which these conversations can happen safely.

7. PET PROJECTS

Has your work gone unexamined for some time? Do you have "pet" projects that you feel protective of when others ask questions? It may be easier to spot others' pet projects than your own. This section guides you to think about your work in a way that will keep it fresh and generate curiosity. It also offers strategies for avoiding the trap of persisting with a pet project that may no longer add value.

People, projects, and styles of work that seem to be immune to criticism are often referred to as "pet projects." We see it in the workplace often: The boss's favorite project that no one dares to question. A coworker who reports to a relative and isn't held accountable. A colleague whose "under the gun" work style puts everyone in a tailspin.

Working around a pet project leaves others feeling frustrated and powerless. At the extreme, these kinds of projects can increase turnover and derail careers. At minimum, they reflect poorly on a leader who is unaware that they are perceived as having one.

In Marshall Goldsmith and Mark Reiter's book *What Got You Here Won't Get You There* (2007), readers are challenged to consider that the work styles and habits that were effective for us in the past may no longer serve us as we progress in our leadership journey. Most of us can easily identify invulnerable styles and habits in *others*. But what about our own "untouchable" people, projects, and styles of work? You might be surprised to realize that you have some. Most of us do. An Alcoholics Anonymous slogan advises, "Don't take *other people's* inventory." We are better served to think about how we might be getting in our own way. Taking an inventory of our own untouchable beliefs and practices is a good place to start.

Think about *why* we have pet projects. They may have a positive origin:

- We are passionate about certain projects or beliefs.
- We appreciate what others can do that we cannot.
- We want to make our mark.
- We desire to make the best use of our strong suits.

But many of us lose perspective over time. These strategies can help you when that happens:

- **Maintain your passion but look for and listen to data** that show when it might be time to try something different. Passion is a powerful motivator and strength, but it is not sufficient to get the results needed for an organization to succeed. Think "passion with a plan" (that includes markers of when things are not working) and genuine buy-in from others. Do you have both?
- **Continue to recruit those who can do what you can't.** This is one way to build a strong team. While doing so, be careful that you are not abdicating your responsibilities to avoid work that you don't like or fear you can't do. You may end up allowing underperformance in another area of an employee's job performance because of the special function that person handles for you. If you find yourself defending an employee, consider whether you are making allowances for one person that you wouldn't make for another.
- **Do work that makes a difference!** Remember that most legacies are not a solo act, especially in healthcare. If you have a pet project, staff your team with people who will be honest with you about when change is needed. As a leader, you have to assume that it is difficult for many people to walk up to you and say, "Hey you know that

project that you are so stoked about? We think it is a risky idea and it is time to end it." Thank people who help you and who take the risk to share a different point of view.

- **Know and use your strengths, but recognize that your strengths may be someone else's headache.** Write a paragraph about your work style and habits. Then, ask someone you work with and trust to write a paragraph about your work style and habits. Where do the two lists line up? Where do they diverge? Both of you might describe you as someone who is creative and who delivers. However, your colleague may see that your creativity often results in last-minute changes, which, in turn, has a negative effect on the workflow of others, causing stress and uncertainty.

A college administrator friend told me that he had once been a dirt bike racer. His group's motto was "If you aren't crashing, you're not trying." When we can't question something, or humbly admit that we need to adapt, it creates bottlenecks in the workplace and stifles innovation. Thank the people who question you—they will help prevent you from being part of that bottleneck.

8. FEAR

Are you sometimes overwhelmed by fear? The world is uncertain, but we can learn to manage the energy we devote to fear. This section offers a technique for facing fear directly and questions that will help you understand how you respond to fear. Read this section to learn ways to accept living with the unknown.

Peter Drucker, the organizational change pioneer and guru, once said, "The best way to predict the future is to create it." Really, Mr. Drucker? If he were alive today, we could ask him how leaders can look ahead with power and fearlessness amid all the uncertainty.

The unknown is a breeding ground for fear. How do we start to untangle the complex changes in healthcare payment systems, population health, the opioid crisis, novel viruses, and so on? Will our organization survive the next five years? Will my job be relevant when the dust settles, and if not, where will I land?

We need to build resilience—the ability to bounce back from ongoing challenges. Don't let fear take over. Turn it on its head with some FEAR-busting practices.

F—Flexibility. Becoming more flexible and adaptable allows us to weather the "high winds" of change. It is a fundamental leadership—and life—skill to develop. What situations make you dig in your heels, prompting immediate resistance? At times, your "no way" response to a change may be appropriate, but sometimes it is an overreaction to a perceived threat. Learn to recognize what *your own resistance* looks, feels, and sounds like. When you sense a strong negative reaction to a change, stop and ask yourself:

- What is the worst-case scenario, and how will I know it is *really* happening?
- What positive outcomes could result if the change is a good move?
- What need am I afraid won't be met? Do I need to feel competent? Have the regard of others? Belong? Maintain control? Be free to act?
- How can I embrace the change *and* get my needs met?

E—Expectations. Manage your expectations by paying attention to your thinking.

- Listen to your inner monologue when you expect the worst. Replace it with a positive statement: "I expect to learn, succeed, find an opportunity to grow in this challenge, find solutions."
- Think of someone who has handled a change or challenge effectively. What actions did they take? How did that person communicate effectively to improve the situation and get their needs met?
- Manage your "what ifs" by focusing on the present moment and breaking a big change into smaller pieces that you can achieve today.

A—Act. Make a list of your concerns. Next, list the things you can't control and stop dwelling on those things! Tear up the list and throw it away. Make a new list identifying things that you can influence and take action.

R—Relate. To repeat: It's all about relationships, whose quality is a result of communication. Rumors fill communication gaps, breeding mistrust. Take these steps with your team:

- **Proactively address rumors.** A good practice is to regularly ask, "What are the rumors flying around? Let's get them out into the open and I'll address them." Earn the reputation for being honest, walking your talk, and promptly following up on questions and concerns.
- **Practice empathy.** It is human to struggle with change. Empathy for others is how we survive. Empathy does not sound like this: "I know it's a stupid initiative, but senior leadership says we have to do it." Instead, it sounds like this: "I understand this is hard, and there are some downsides. We will monitor the problems and benefits, and we can only do that if we all give 100 percent. I need your best effort, and I will do the same."

9. HELPING TOO MUCH

Are you really, really helpful? Does helping others make you feel good? These are not trick questions! Helping others is admirable, but sometimes we help too much, undermining our own and others' efforts. This section explores how much helping is too much, how too much helping affects you, and alternatives to helping that actually *do* help.

Compassion is taking action to alleviate suffering. When leaders seek to help their employees, they are engaging in an act of compassion.

"Compassion is not a relationship between the healer and the wounded. It's a relationship between equals."

—Pema Chodron

Helping is ingrained in our culture as the right thing to do—and I agree! Being of service is central to the framework of the servant leader (Greenleaf Center for Servant Leadership 2020) and a bedrock of true leadership. "It is better to give than to receive" is a touchstone that most leaders have grown up hearing, encouraging them to bring their heart to their work and to do "for" others. You might hear it in comments such as "I don't ask others to do anything I won't do" or "I don't want to burden my staff because they are already so busy." These sentiments are well intentioned, originating from a desire for fairness. However, it is wise to consider that sometimes helping may leave people feeling unequal. Sometimes, you may be helping too much.

> **You miss the forest for the trees.** People want you to lead—that is why you are in a leadership role. But you will have a hard time leading strategically if you are always filling in for others. Reflect on how much of your time is spent doing the

job you were promoted from. Working managers have to do this sometimes, but it can become the default. This trap is deceptively easy to fall into because it satisfies the need to do work that makes us feel competent. **Instead:** Get support for your leadership role to learn the new skills you need to be successful. Understand and accept that there is a learning curve, and it's normal to feel unsure of yourself at times. Face the discomfort of the unknown. You will eventually learn your new roles and skills, but only if you are willing to be uncomfortable for a while.

Employees miss opportunities to learn. Just as you are struggling through your own learning curve, your employees must do that, too. We want to make it easier for them, but who are we to say that an employee doesn't need this very struggle to grow into the person they are meant to be? Who has not learned from a challenging situation? When we take over someone else's struggle rather than helping, we run the risk of getting in the way of growth. **Instead:** Resist the urge to step in and rescue them. Show support by facilitating employees' learning through their own discomfort.

Employees may believe you don't trust them, leading to disengagement. Your employees feel empowered when they know you trust them. If you are too quick to take over rather than empowering staff, you may be unintentionally sending a message: "I know better; you can't be trusted to figure this out." **Instead:** Extend trust, first by reminding yourself that others are capable, too.

Others will respond to your offer to pitch in with "Awesome, it's yours!" You may feel virtuous for a while, but then you will notice that employees are taking vacation days and shouldering a lighter load, while you never take a day off or leave on time. If you are feeling overwhelmed, overworked, or becoming resentful, these may be signs that you are helping too quickly and too often. Remember, we teach people how to treat us. **Instead:** Respond to a request for help with inquiry:

- "What ideas do you have to solve the problem?"
- "What would you do if you couldn't reach me?"
- "I can't cover this for you. Work with your team to come up with alternative solutions."

Being a good leader and manager *is* helping.

10. RECEIVING FEEDBACK GRACEFULLY

> **When you hear negative feedback about your work, do your defenses kick in?** This happens to the best of us, even when we say that we welcome feedback. This section gives you ten tips for managing your reaction in the moment so that you can hear the feedback and use it to your best advantage.

It's not always easy to be on the receiving end of feedback. Delivering it is hard enough! Even when the person giving you feedback does so with skill and tact, tough feedback can come as a surprise. The receiver senses a threat to their freedom, their sense of competence or control. Delivering and hearing difficult feedback can result in hurt feelings and misunderstandings.

When we are fearful or angry, we stop listening and start justifying, missing the wisdom that is before us. The following tips will help you consciously manage yourself in challenging moments and accept the benefit of feedback:

- **Breathe.** One of the first things that many of us do when we feel threatened is to stop breathing deeply or even hold our breath. Less oxygen to the brain limits our ability to act thoughtfully. We need to breathe to calm ourselves. Practice conscious breathing by exhaling every bit of air you can and then inhaling deeply a couple of times. You will be able to hear better.

- **"Tell me more."** Instead of jumping to explain or justify, say "Tell me more." This response gives you time to learn more about the real issue, seek specific examples to better understand the concern, and manage your response.

- **Ask for time.** If your defenses are kicking up, it may not be the best time to start a dialogue. Instead, ask to meet later. For example, "Discussing what you have to share is important to me. I have another obligation right now, but can we meet in half an hour?"

- **Thank the person giving the feedback.** Especially if you are in a higher-level position, and even if you are not happy to hear what the person has to say, say thank you. This keeps communication open for the future. Feedback can be a gift if we are open to seeing it that way. Saying thank you helps us remember that.

- **Remind yourself** that you want to be effective, to grow, and to learn. All information is useful to that end. In thoughtfully considering the feedback you receive, you will learn more about your impact on others.

- **It's OK to say "This is hard to hear."** It is a misconception that leaders must always appear tough. To build trust, we must show vulnerability. Does the feedback make you feel vulnerable or exposed? How you demonstrate authentically that you are taking a tough message to heart can show the other person that you care and that you are willing to reflect on the message.

- **Assume good intent.** We often jump to make assumptions. The only helpful assumption is that "This person has my best interest in mind and wants what is best for me." Take a short walk and stop spinning stories about the other person's intentions. Assuming the worst is a no-win approach.

- **Listen actively.** Do you want to be a more skillful communicator? Listen better. Reflect what you heard to make sure you are understanding correctly.
- **Ask for more feedback regularly,** especially if you are a leader. You will get used to receiving feedback, which takes out some of the sting. Receiving feedback regularly will help you learn and gain the respect of your team. You can't fix what you don't know about!
- **Extend trust.** Even if you do not trust the person delivering the feedback, bring trust to the front of your mind. Trust in yourself to manage your emotions; trust that something good can come from a difficult conversation; trust that you will get through whatever comes of this feedback, because you have gotten through other difficult things and grown from them.

11. BREAD, THE STAFF OF LEADERSHIP

Would you like some tips on how to be great even while you are learning? Using bread baking as a metaphor, this section offers tips on accepting yourself where you are as you develop your leadership skills.

"Bread is the staff of life" is the notion that bread is essential to life. It sustains us. Leadership growth is also essential to continue to achieve results. I have enjoyed moments of great pride and endured humbling failures both in bread baking and in leadership roles. The way these two endeavors come together offers interesting opportunities to learn.

Flops can be useful. The classic cookbook *Laurel's Kitchen Bread Book* (Robertson 1984) suggests starting with a "learning loaf." You know up front that your loaf might turn out like a hockey puck. Whatever the results, take the opportunity to analyze what went wrong and what went right and apply that learning to the next attempt. *Leaders:* High achievers may expect that things will not go as planned as you grow in leadership. Embrace a little failure. Drill into mixed results to see what you can learn (rather than beating yourself up or giving up). The next attempt will go better if you stay open to the lesson.

A task is only daunting because you haven't learned it yet. Although my ego enjoys impressing you with my weekly bread baking brag, don't be so impressed. It's easy once you know how. *Leaders:* Remember that you once had to learn all the skills you have mastered. Think of something you know how to do that you didn't know five years ago. Remind yourself that other people intimidate you only when you give them permission to do so. Keep learning.

A mentor match is a great nudge. Hearing a radio interview about bread baking is what finally motivated me to try it again. *Leaders:* What is your preferred learning style? We use all of our senses to learn, but most of us prefer one way of learning, whether it be auditory, visual, or kinesthetic. Seek a mentor who matches up with the way you learn best.

Baking is chemistry. People have been baking bread for centuries, but when new scientific data is learned, we need to adapt. The way I bake bread is different—and easier—than the way my mom did it because bakers have experimented and taken risks in the intervening years. *Leaders:* We wouldn't think of practicing medicine the same way we did 50 years ago, so why wouldn't we adapt to best practices in leadership? Push back on theories—even what you read here—and think critically. Stay curious and push your mentors to adapt, too.

Sometimes simpler is better. Purists may chafe at my shortcuts, but my bread tastes fabulous. *Leaders:* You may be making things more complicated than they have to be. Are you sometimes frustrated that people don't seem to understand what you want from them, or they are less engaged in your initiatives than you hoped? Look for ways to simplify instructions, jargon, processes, steps, and communication.

Start with a "recipe." Back to bread chemistry: I learned the basics from experienced bakers and recipes. Then I began to experiment with my own ingredients and flavors. *Leaders:* Establish a firm foundation of leadership skills. Use tools (recipes) for coaching, leading change, resolving conflict, communicating effectively, and so on. These skills are different from the ones you learned before you were promoted to a manager role. Like baking, once you have learned the basics, you can add your own flair. No leader is exactly like you.

Establish habits. I bake bread just about every weekend. Keeping up this habit makes it second nature to me. *Leaders:* Practice the essential skills regularly. Have difficult coaching conversations. Check in with the person you'd rather avoid. Make the skill you want to improve a recurring appointment on your calendar, so that it gets easier with practice and becomes a part of what you do and who you are.

Imagine success. Nothing smells or tastes better than a warm, freshly baked loaf of bread. The feeling of pride when it turns out well inspires confidence to try more. *Leaders:* Confidence comes from outside your comfort zone, not from within it. Whatever leadership challenge scares you, first envision success with all of your senses.

Finesse what is good to make it consistently great. A simple switch, from measuring flour with a measuring cup to weighing it on a scale, improved my results from really good to consistently great. *Leaders:* Where do your skills need tweaking? Though it is true that bread baking requires balancing many variables, it is never as messy as people are. Your coaching skills may not have consistent outcomes because each employee's situation is unique, but *you* can become a force to count on, teaching people what they can expect from you. Your consistency is a key component of building team trust.

If you want to tackle bread successfully, read "My Mother's Peasant Bread" at Alexandra's Kitchen (Stafford 2012), and you'll be turning out beautiful loaves in no time.

12. TAKE A BREAK FROM GUILT

Do you ever feel guilty when you have done nothing wrong? Guilt is a big energy drain for many leaders. This section explores the reasons behind guilt, how it has served you, and alternatives that could serve you better.

Are you willing to give up some of your guilt? It may be a habit that you are more attached to than you are willing to admit. Do you feel guilty in any of these situations?

- You say no to a request
- You delegate a task or project
- You see someone else struggling
- You choose to rest (take a lunch, vacation, break, nap)
- You do something just for fun, especially when . . .
- You see that others are working

"I should _____" is a worn-out path to guilt that suggests you are falling short and punishing yourself for it. But guilt offers only the *illusion* that you are holding yourself accountable. You are putting yourself in guilt jail without looking at the facts of your case.

Leaders often spend an inordinate—and unproductive—amount of time and energy feeling guilty. But you don't have to. Guilty feelings start with your thoughts. Effective leaders reflect, examining their beliefs in the light of day, and then take action. Consider the following ideas to help you do that:

Access to energy. Think of something you feel guilty about and imagine: If I didn't feel guilty about this, what kind of energy would be available to me? What goals might I be energized to pursue if guilt were not weighing me down? Does this guilt serve any purpose?

Reality check. What exactly do you feel guilty about? Guilt is about wrongdoing. What did you do wrong? Speak the facts only. "I delegated work to someone, and because I was not clear about my expectations, the person failed." Identifying facts clearly without melodrama should take about a minute. Is your experience of guilt in proportion to the "crime?"

Amend and apologize appropriately. Spend your energy on learning to get it right next time. Apologize when doing so is appropriate. For example, "This delegation did not go as well as it could have. I take responsibility for not being clearer in my expectations. I will to do better next time by using this delegation form with you so that we're on the same page." Then move on. (Amend and apologize does not apply to fixing things you did not do wrong, such as taking a lunch break.)

Let go and grow. This can be tough. If you feel guilty when others struggle, consider that it may insulting to others that you want to take over for them. Allow people the learning they are entitled to. When you can't let go, ask yourself, "What am I hanging on to? What do I have control over?

What am I afraid of losing if I let go, and is that likely? And if it is likely, does it matter? What would be the benefits to the other person if I could let this go?"

Capacity for trust. Do you unconsciously cling to guilt because you believe that only you can hold things together, get the work done, be responsible? This is unfair to others. You might think that you are protecting others, but really you are saying, "I don't trust you; only I can be trusted." Guilt can also reflect a lack of trust in yourself. Say, "I trust myself to know when I need to take a break, say no, stop helping; I trust that I will survive if others don't like it."

Making choices. Have you had the experience of making a choice for yourself, then being unable to enjoy it because you felt guilty? Consider that both of these statements are true: You are not indispensable, but you are important enough to deserve good things.

Be humble. Guilt may stem from the fear that if we set limits, care for ourselves, say no, and delegate confidently, others will think we are "too much." Wallowing in guilt is not the way to prove humility. Role model humility by thanking and recognizing others genuinely, showing vulnerability, valuing the expertise of others, and asking for help.

CHAPTER 7

Difficult Conversations and Coaching

DIFFICULT CONVERSATIONS ARE never easy, nor should we expect them to be, because they involve honesty, vulnerability, and risk. But the cost of avoiding difficult conversations is high, and the outcomes, when handled with skill and the right intentions, can be life-changing. Revisit this chapter as often as you need to.

SELF-ASSESSMENT SCORING:

1—I am struggling with or not yet skilled at this.

2—I am starting to work on improving at this, but I need more skill building.

3—I am making some consistent progress in improving at this.

4—I am doing very well in this area.

Determine your current level of skill on these coaching competencies (score 1–4):

1. I confidently address underperformance concerns even when the employee is a friend. Score: _____

2. I skillfully give feedback to employees who display arrogance to help them see themselves more clearly and influence their behavior. Score: _____

3. I do not get in the middle of others' conflicts; instead, I help resolve conflicts using tools that are appropriate to the situation. Score: _____

4. The people who report to me feel comfortable giving me tough feedback. I have intentionally created a safe environment that fosters this kind of interaction. Score: _____

5. I give feedback that is clear and specific without labeling or judging, so that the person receiving the feedback knows exactly what I expect. Score: _____

6. I understand the tenets of leading successful change and employ them systematically in my change initiatives. Score: _____

7. I can discern how much time is appropriate for coaching a performance issue, and I have a plan for consistently communicating with my team about coaching. Score: _____

Now explore the corresponding sections that follow to learn how to improve skills that need work or enhance your current skills.

1. CONFLICT OR COACHING?

Are you uncomfortable addressing job performance issues with employees? Sometimes you may have a unique relationship with an employee—perhaps you are friends—but other factors play a role, too. Read this section to learn how to say what needs to be said. Explore why you feel uncomfortable addressing job performance issues and how to overcome your discomfort.

Sometimes leaders ask me to help resolve a conflict with an employee when in fact there is no conflict. What is really needed is a coaching conversation. Conflict involves emotions, competing needs, and different viewpoints. When coaching an employee about a performance problem, particularly when it is related to something we are passionate about, it is easy to confuse conflict and coaching.

Coaching is a relationship that supports the growth and development of others. When you coach others, you want to listen to and look at them to help them discover what they are capable of and what they need to do to reach their goals. Coaching plays a critical role in leadership: You must be willing to see the potential in others and help them to see it, too. Reinforcing positive behavior is a rewarding part of coaching. But addressing tough issues such as poor job performance, behavioral problems, or failure to meet expectations can be uncomfortable. Both, however, are part of your coaching responsibility.

- **Discomfort that feels like conflict sometime occurs because you have a personal friendship with an employee.** In that case, acknowledge the discomfort. You both know it is uncomfortable; just say so. "We need to talk about your job performance. This is uncomfortable because we are friends. But our friendship only makes me more committed to helping you succeed and doing what I can in my role as your manager to support you."
- **If you are squirming because you didn't always follow the rules before you became a manager,** admit your error and share what you have learned. "You're right; I didn't always follow this policy in the past. I want to tell you what I have learned, why I am now committed to this policy, and why I am asking you to follow it as well." Sometimes people don't follow policies because they don't make sense until the dots are connected. In

your leadership role, you can and should help employees connect the dots.

- **If you are angry with employees who are not doing what they should be doing,** examine the origin of your anger. An employee's issues and performance are not personal. Reread that last sentence for emphasis. What stories are you telling yourself about an employee? What kinds of judgments are you making? How might you view the situation if you weren't angry? Step back from these stories and judgments. Examine exactly what has happened and your expectations going forward—without emotion. It's not personal, it's performance. Approach the coaching conversation *after* you have sorted this out.

Whether you are engaged in conflict resolution or coaching, ask yourself, "What part of this do I own?" Have you tolerated poor performance in the past? Have you neglected to follow up on a performance issue? Were your instructions misunderstood? Take responsibility for what is within your control.

2. ARROGANCE

Are you coaching someone whom you would describe as arrogant? This section offers ideas on how to address specific behaviors, give constructive feedback, and offer employees tools that will help them achieve what they really want in a way that builds rather than divides a team.

"Early in life I had to choose between honest arrogance and hypocritical humility. I chose the former and have seen no reason to change."

—Frank Lloyd Wright

Wisconsin's famous architect Frank Lloyd Wright had a very different work environment than healthcare professionals today. Arrogance in healthcare can derail a career. Smart, talented, and often right, arrogant leaders use body language that scares some people and invites fights with others. They often share little about themselves, and they don't invite others to do so, which can send the signal that they are not interested in the team. They interrupt, state conclusions, and shut down others who disagree with them. These kinds of behaviors stall teamwork—and increasingly, teamwork is the way we get things done.

Arrogance presents two challenges in coaching:

- Unlike Wright, the arrogant person may not see themselves as arrogant.
- The very nature of unpleasant arrogant behaviors makes others reluctant to address them.

Do you need to coach someone who may not know or care that they are seen as arrogant? Rather than trying to convince someone of their own arrogance, which will prompt defensiveness in most people, focus on behavioral skills.

Start with nonverbal awareness. We are responsible for the visual cues we send out. First, describe the cues that you see consistently (frowning, raising an eyebrow when others speak, staring, pursed lips, smirking, tapping fingers or feet, etc.). Then, describe the behaviors that you would like to see instead (lean in, open facial expression, intermittent versus solid or no eye contact, a genuine smile, etc.). If possible, record a meeting and watch the recording together to facilitate the discussion about the employee's demeanor.

Who is the employee comfortable with? The employee may loosen up around certain people. Perhaps they laugh a little or share some of the things they are interested in outside of work. Ask the employee to describe how their behavior and demeanor are different in those environments and to work at assuming that posture with others.

Teach the employee to "read" others. If you can record a meeting, do you see people verbally or even physically "backing up" from this employee? Coworkers might interact with others in the group but avoid responding to the arrogant person. Discuss the reactions of others in the group as a learning discussion, not a finger-pointing exercise. Share your observations about how others respond to the employee. Encourage the employee to adopt an inquiry approach with people who tend to back away from them (e.g., "I'm interested in your point of view; what are your ideas?"). Suggest the employee intentionally check in with the group during meetings. For example, "Can we pause here and check in? I want to make sure that I'm not dominating the discussion and that everyone has a chance to weigh in and address the issues that are important to all of us."

Five-second rule. During a discussion or debate, ask the employee to wait five seconds after someone has finished speaking before they respond. Five seconds might seem like forever, but this technique can heighten awareness of interrupting or "conclusion-stating" behavior.

Value the employee's knowledge. Remind the employee that their knowledge is valuable. However, when others feel dismissed, no one wins. Smart is not enough when collaboration is the working model.

3. FAQ: HOW DO I GET OUT OF THE MIDDLE?

Have you landed in the middle of others' conflict? This is one of the most common challenges I hear from leaders. This section offers strategies for staying out of employee conflicts in the first place and encouraging employees to resolve conflicts independently.

A frequently asked question in leadership workshops is "How do I help the employee who is having a conflict with a coworker and expects me to solve it? I feel like I am stuck in the middle." Often, an employee will refuse to even talk to the coworker they are in conflict with. The employee may have many justifications for that refusal:

- "I could never talk to them; they would blow up at me and make my life miserable with the others on the team."
- "I've tried and it didn't work."
- "They are like this with everyone; no one else is willing to come to tell you about it."
- "Isn't this your job as the manager?"
- All frequently accompanied by, "Don't tell them that I talked to you about this!"

You've just gotten yourself into a trap. You might ask yourself why this keeps happening. What am I getting out of this? (Feeling needed? Avoiding a difficult conversation myself?) What role am I playing in this drama? (Savior?) Have I fully accepted my leader role, or do I feel torn between being a part of the team and being a leader? (Feeling rejected?)

How do you get out of the middle of an employee conflict—or, better yet, avoid the trap in the first place?

Refuse to listen to one side privately. Listening to only one side of a conflict unfairly influences our view of the situation. When a conversation goes down this road, bring the other person into the discussion immediately.

Be cautious about allowing venting. Venting about frustrations of a busy day is one thing. A complaint session about a particular coworker is not venting, it is gossip, and allowing it says that we think gossip is OK. When an employee is "venting," use the conversation to teach that venting has a negative influence. Ask the employee to shift into a problem-solving mode to be a positive influence.

It is not enough to tell employees, "You have to talk to the person yourself." Saying this is akin to telling a nonclinical employee "You have to put that IV in the patient" because it is what is needed. We must teach people the skills they need to have difficult conversations and provide plenty of support before and after the conversation. Consider how hard it is for most of us to have difficult conversations even *with* training!

Resist the urge to "collude" with the complainer. You may feel just as frustrated as your employee. The "complainer" may be your friend. This gives you all the more reason to set clear boundaries by refusing to team up with one employee against another. Pay attention to subtle ways of doing this, too. It's not only our words that speak. Friends often share nonverbal cues, such as a "knowing look" or a raised eyebrow. A tone of voice that implies an unspoken agreement, even if your words say otherwise, will undermine your credibility.

Increase your presence. Sometimes we are so focused on our work that we miss what is going on right under our noses. Notice the interactions among your team. Coach employees to reinforce the behaviors you want to see. Make sure your team doesn't have to come to you with job performance problems that are happening under your watch, not theirs.

Have a discussion with the whole team. For example, "I am committed to helping you sort out conflicts that come up on the team. To best help you, when you have a concern about a coworker, here's what I expect." Then lay out some options:

- Try to work it out among yourselves.

- If you can't work it out, or don't know how to say what you want to say, come to me for coaching practice. I will expect you to leave our discussion and talk to your coworker as we practiced. I will follow up to make sure you have held the discussion.

- If talking with your coworker doesn't seem possible, ask me to set up a meeting so that I can facilitate a discussion between the two of you. I will help you both get your message across and come up with a workable plan. I will follow up with both of you after this discussion to make sure that you are taking action on your plan.

- Do not come to me with problems that you don't intend to follow through on. This may sound as if I am not willing to help. That is not the case. When I am put in the middle of a conflict, it is unfair to the person you are in conflict with, it ties my hands by not allowing me to give specific feedback, and it damages trust among our team. I am fully committed to helping you in the ways I have described here—which doesn't include anyone talking behind someone else's back.

4. DEAR CEO

How do you encourage people to give you feedback without their being intimidated by your leadership position? You can't fix what you don't know about. This section offers guideposts for creating an environment in which people feel comfortable giving you honest feedback.

Who do CEOs trust to tell them when they are not coming across well? I suppose a spouse or a paid consultant might be willing to say "That speech? It was really off the mark." As a leader, whether a frontline manager or a CEO, you can enhance your performance by encouraging candid feedback about how you come across to others. Perception is everything, and other people's perceptions can surprise us sometimes. We are better off knowing and understanding how we are perceived so that we can address our shortcomings.

Imagine being told that you:

- Exhibit behaviors that undermine the organization's ground rules for meetings (you arrive late to meetings, take phone calls or text during meetings, have side conversations, etc.).
- Set high standards for customer service but neglect to greet staff in the hall.
- Announce an open door policy but are rarely available and don't have an open chair in your office.
- Ask for input, but when others share their concerns or disagreements, you become defensive or irritated.
- Promote direct communication but then make negative comments about staff who are not present.
- Regularly exhibit behaviors such as eye rolling or interrupting.

Often we do not even realize we are doing these things, but leaders are carefully observed by staff. Employees notice the little things—both good and bad. Leaders may underestimate the extent to which their behaviors influence others.

Giving difficult feedback to someone who is higher on the chain of command can be intimidating. Staff may feel the risk is too great. Consider the following approaches to encourage staff to give you honest feedback. Whatever your personality style, the goal is to make sure people perceive you as accessible.

- **Ask for feedback.** Use formal mechanisms such as surveys but also, more importantly, informal methods, such as asking for input after a meeting you have led. Ask staff to tell you one thing that you did well and one thing that you could do better next time. People notice your behaviors and your words and interpret them through their own filters. Open dialogue can clarify these interpretations.

- **Openly announce your intent.** Sometimes feedback conversations go badly when you feel threatened by the other person's intentions (e.g., the employee intends to cause trouble or just doesn't like you). Announce that your intent in seeking feedback is to simply grow as a leader, to be the best leader you can be. Then assume good intent on the part of employees.

- **Say thank you.** Thank the person who takes the risk to give you feedback, and resist the urge to explain or justify your behaviors or actions. Listen first for what you can learn. For example, you may need to stay connected to email and text messages during meetings, but employees could perceive you as being distracted or inattentive. After hearing this feedback, you might decide to announce at the beginning of a meeting that you will need to check your messages during the meeting for a particular purpose. By doing so, you acknowledge the ground rules up front, and your honest communication removes conjecture about what you might be doing on your phone.

- **Try to change your behavior.** Imagine that an employee takes the risk to confide that you seem to spend more time interacting with particular groups or individuals in the organization, leaving others feeling overlooked. Chances are, you weren't aware of doing anything that looked like favoritism. Ramp up your management by walking around. Go out of your way to connect with employees in different areas of the building, and engage with staff you don't know well to learn more about their work or their hobbies.

5. ATTITUDE ADJUSTMENT—AND A METHOD FOR FEEDBACK

> **Do you need to address an employee's attitude but don't know what to say?** This section gives you a method for discussing behaviors of concern and clearly stating what you want to see instead.

When you talk to an employee about their attitude, you need to be specific about what concerns you and explain what you want instead. For example, telling an employee "I'd like to see a more positive attitude from you" is unlikely to be effective because it does not convey clear expectations going forward.

What are the specific behaviors that you see, hear, or otherwise observe that lead you to believe that someone has a bad attitude? The following are some behaviors that suggest a negative attitude:

- Eye rolling
- Slumping or turning away from a speaker
- Frowning
- Failing to greet others or mumbling a greeting
- Refusing to look up from work to acknowledge someone who has entered a room or common area
- Sighing
- Raising eyebrows at someone else's comment or behavior but not saying anything
- Speaking in a monotonous or excessively loud tone of voice or emphasizing certain words to get your attention
- Staying quiet when asked for input or working on other things during a meeting
- Holding side conversations during meetings
- Refusing to offer to help others when needed

- Muttering under the breath
- Failing to take the initiative to look for what else needs to be done

Coaching begins by adjusting your own attitude. Tell yourself, "I want the people I lead to be successful. My job is to mirror back to them what I see to help them realize the impact they have." Here is a simple coaching framework, followed by an example:

- **State your purpose.** "I would like to talk with you about some things I have observed that may be getting in the way of your success."
- **State the specific behavior you want to address.** "I've notice that during the last several staff meetings, you sat turned away from others. You didn't make eye contact or speak up when asked for input."
- **State the effect of the behavior.** "When you don't show interest through your body language or through participation in the discussion, you bring down the mood of the team, making others feel as if you are not on board with our work."
- **State the behavior you want to see instead.** "I'd like to see you join the conversation and share your ideas, even if you disagree. I'd like you to sit up at the table and make more eye contact with the team."
- **State the expected result of the new behavior.** "When I see you participating more, it gives me confidence that we are working as a team to reach our goals. Others will see this, too, and will trust you as a team member. I want that for you."
- **Ask questions.** "What do you think?" This opens the door for dialogue.

This framework works well in giving feedback, which can be uncomfortable for many. Often, feedback is lacking in these ways:

- It is too abrupt, setting up the receiver to get defensive.
- It is too vague, leaving the receiver unclear about what we expect
- It is too uncomfortable, as concern about hurting someone's feelings leaves important things unsaid.
- It is given to a group broadly rather than to the individual who needs to hear it, resulting in high performers feeling chastised and the low performer potentially missing it entirely.

Explaining the purpose of the feedback establishes why you are holding the conversation. Then, articulate the behavior you want to see, the effect of that behavior, the change in behavior that you are asking for, and the desired results. Here are two more performance examples that might resonate with you:

Behavior: I notice . . .

- "When you come to meetings, you frequently do not have materials you need and have to leave to get things you forgot."
- "Your perfume fills up the workspace we share."

Effect: The effect is . . .

- "When you have to leave the meeting, we start late and get behind on the project."
- "I am getting headaches from the perfume due to my allergies."

Ask: I am asking . . .

- "You to be on time for meetings with all the required materials on hand."
- "If we could talk about some alternatives to the use of perfume."

Result: Because then . . .

- "Our meeting time will be more productive and efficient, and your team members will have more confidence in your dedication to the work."
- "We can both feel honored for our individuality and needs in making this a good work space for both of us."

Remember to follow up by asking, "What do you think?"

Can you come up with another example? It takes courage to hold these conversations, but it is worth it. Be courageous!

6. LEADING CHANGE Q&A

Are you experiencing resistance to a change? Would you like some ideas on addressing challenges when leading change? Read these questions posed by leaders like you for tips and opportunities to reflect on your role in leading change.

When you are leading change, you can expect to hit some bumps in the road. The following list is a collection of questions from a group of new leaders—maybe some of the same questions that you have—along with some answers for you to consider.

How can I get my manager or higher-ups to buy into a change and be accountable for a behavior? It takes guts to coach up the ladder, but remember that your leader wants to be successful, too. Could you show them how a behavior or a change could make them look good? A couple of questions to ask: "How could I help you with this? What would it take to get your support? What would you need to see or know to give this a try?"

How can I get veteran employees to go along with a change? Employees who have been with an organization for a long time often like things the way they are because they feel competent. Losing a sense of competence can be threatening. Acknowledge this fear while reassuring veteran employees that you will train and support them in the new way. Ask them to "pilot" the new way for a while to identify the snags so that you can really evaluate it. Say, "I need your support and experience. Your modeling the new way for others will help us be successful."

How do I enforce the new way without being a "cop?" Catch employees getting it right and reinforce the new behavior: "That is exactly what I wanted to see, great work!" If a problem arises, rather than recite the rule, ask employees how they understand your expectations. If they can't articulate your expectations correctly, that tells you what needs to be clarified. Ask what they need from you to succeed going forward. Listen for underlying needs and doubts. Too often, we underestimate others' learning curves. Find the early adopters and supporters and ask for their help to lead the way. You can't change anything alone. Sometimes you will have to address underperformance.

What if I am upholding a change that has been implemented, but my peers are not following it with their staff? My team feels it is unfair. It is more than unfair—it is a morale killer. Talk to the individual leader and share the impact of their actions on your team. Ask what it would take to get their buy-in. Bring the question to your leadership team and hash it out openly. Don't leave the room until everyone says "I'm in" or "I still have questions" and all of them are answered.

How do I move a change forward when it stalls? Revisit your vision of what you want from the change. Ask whether people are clear about where you are headed. If not, you may need to reenergize the team around the ultimate goal. What is at stake if you don't change? You may need to remind people of the sense of urgency. Even a desired change can stall if there is little consequence for slowing down.

How do I hardwire a change? Reinforce successes. Tell stories about how the change will make a difference or how it will lead to something better. Find ways to make it easier to do things the new way than the old way. Remind those who are overwhelmed of other changes they have navigated successfully. Ask people how they are doing with the change, what they are learning, where they still need help (and make it happen), and what is getting in their way (and move it out of the way).

How do I manage many new changes and keep up with the current workload? How much change is too much change? This is a tough question. In short, when a new change is initiated, it is fair to ask for a change project plan. This plan should identify the urgency, vision, stakeholders, team members needed, time frame for milestones, role clarification, work time estimate, and scope (what is included and what is not). It is fair to ask how the new change fits in with existing priorities. Don't set yourself up for failure and overload yourself by saying yes before you know what you are saying yes to.

How do I "sell" a change that I can't buy into myself? Go to the decision makers in your organizations and be honest. You might say, "I need help understanding this change from my employees' perspective. I want to support the organization's direction, but to be able to do that, I need more information about why we are doing this, how it will impact people, what will improve because of it, and what is at stake if we are not successful." Even if you are not fully on board with the change, resist the temptation to throw the organization or administration under the bus when you present the change to your team. Doing so will likely backfire on you. Sometimes you simply have to communicate that a change, even if it is unpleasant, must be embraced. Let your team know, "We need to use our best effort and talent to make this change successful. If we give it our all and it still doesn't work, then we'll deal with that. But we won't know unless we give it our best."

I have some staff who are on board with the change but others who are lagging behind. How do I engage everyone? You don't need 100 percent buy-in to get the ball rolling. Those who are on board with the change will create momentum that will help you bring the others along. Find opportunities to recognize and reward supporters. Point out how they are getting results. Ask those who are reluctant what they need to get on board. Be sure you are clearly signaling that change is not optional.

How do I address unrealistic fears about what could go wrong? While it may be tempting to dismiss fears as irrational, doing so will not assuage the fearful. Instead, help employees explore the worst-case scenario and discuss red flags to watch out for and possible solutions if the worst comes to pass. Ask employees to watch for those red flags and keep you informed as you move forward. Pick several data markers that will make these fears more objective.

How can I lead a change if my primary stakeholders won't even go to meetings? Maybe you can't. Hold off on making a change until you have the commitment of your key stakeholders, or else you may find yourself spinning your wheels. If you do get commitment but meeting attendance is still a problem, ask for alternative means of communication. Does everyone need to attend every meeting? Create a communication matrix that identifies communication goals (why), methods (how—meeting? email? quick huddle updates?), and outcomes (what and when), and use it throughout the project.

How do I implement a change in behavior when it should already be happening? Life and leadership are all about having skillful conversations that you wish weren't necessary. If you are thinking "This is common sense," remember that *common* means you are assuming agreement. Others' sense of what is right may not be in agreement with yours. Be explicit about what you are looking for.

How do I maintain momentum in a long-term change project? No one can stay motivated forever without feedback or reinforcement. You must plan for and build in early and recurring successes. These wins won't announce themselves; propose them as part of your project plan. Celebrate milestones along the way toward the ultimate goal. Engage your team at the beginning of the project to identify those milestones (when you hit certain targets, achieve specific goals, etc.).

How often should I follow up with my team to see how they are doing with a change project? There is no "one size fits all" in following up, but you can't abdicate all responsibility once you have delegated it. You might ask, "How would I know if you were struggling? Halfway through? Running into roadblocks? In need of my help or support?"

So much of what makes change successful has to do with skillful communication and solid project management. Work on those two things, and your changes will have a better chance of success.

7. FOLLOWING UP ON FEEDBACK

Has someone come to you with input about another employee's performance and now wants to know how you have acted on their input? Are you unsure how long to coach someone on problem performance? This section focuses on ways to build and maintain trust when you are working with team members on performance issues.

Your team is generally the first to know when there is a performance problem with a coworker. Your solid performers may have even been the ones to make you aware of a problem if you have not seen the behaviors yourself. If there is a problem that you need to address, what do you do if the employee comes back and asks what you are doing to follow up on their feedback?

You want people to trust that you will keep their information confidential, too, if they were ever being coached. This is a good opportunity to reinforce that message: "I want you to trust that any concerns that have been brought to my attention are taken seriously. I can't share information about any conversations I might be having with other employees, any more than I would if you and I were having confidential conversations."

Asking people for their trust is the first step. Making it clear that you will not share confidential information is the second. But then you have to make sure that evidence of your coaching is coming to fruition. When it comes to trusting that you are following up on concerns, your high performers need to see that the problem performance is improving or the low performer is moving on.

Allowing poor performance to continue destroys your ability to hold *anyone* on your team accountable, negatively impacting morale, commitment to the team, and organizational culture. But let's say you are coaching someone to make a change and it's taking some time, with ups and downs along the way. This is where the long view makes a difference. Over time, if your team sees that people are held accountable, they will understand that some changes don't happen overnight—but they do happen.

However, if you have been coaching someone with no consistent progress, ask yourself whether the problem employee's performance is starting to reflect on you and your credibility. Hope is not a performance improvement strategy. There is no "right" amount of time for coaching, and generally we should give people ample opportunity to improve. But do set a time frame for improvement and ask yourself these questions about the employee you are coaching:

- Have you been as clear as possible about what needs to change?
- Are you negotiating a change that is not optional? If something is required, are you talking about it like it is a choice? If so, it is time to take a stand.
- Have you set deadlines for specific improvements?
- Can the employee articulate what is expected?
- What would convince you either to cut your losses or continue coaching? What is the deal breaker either way?
- Does this employee exemplify what you want your team to stand for? If not . . .
- Why is this employee still working for your organization? If you are defending an employee because the position is hard to fill, you may want to reconsider. A warm body isn't better than nobody.

Typically, these sticky situations are not about technical skill deficits. If they are, you can help employees by encouraging them to share their struggles with the team and ask for help. Coach employees on how to seek mentorship effectively, and support your team in creating a mentoring environment by recognizing when you see those behaviors. In this way, employees can share their own progress with the team.

CHAPTER 8

Diversity

DIVERSE TEAMS CAN be strong, but sometimes we do not fully take advantage of those strengths when we focus on differences. There are many types of diversity—this chapter does not begin to cover them all. The topics in this chapter offer insights into broadly applied concepts, as evidenced by the questions in the self-assessment.

SELF-ASSESSMENT SCORING:

1—I am struggling with or not yet skilled at this.

2—I am starting to work on improving at this, but I need more skill building.

3—I am making some consistent progress in improving at this.

4—I am doing very well in this area.

Determine your current level of skill on these diversity competencies (score 1–4):

1. I am respectfully curious and actively interested in learning about people who are different from me. Score: _____

2. I understand my personality type and what I need to reenergize myself. I understand how my personality type affects others. Score: _____

3. I am aware of my own biases and work to address bias in all forms when I see it in others. Score: _____

4. I use critical thinking to pause my biases before I respond and react. Score: _____

5. I can adapt to new ways of thinking in the workplace introduced by people who are different from me. Score: _____

6. I take time to appreciate the gifts that diversity in the workplace brings. Score: _____

7. I lead people as unique individuals instead of making assumptions about them based on stereotypes. Score: _____

Now explore the corresponding sections that follow to learn how to improve skills that need work or enhance your current skills.

1. LET'S TALK ABOUT RELIGION

Are you aware of how talking about your religious beliefs— and assuming that others share them—could make some employees feel excluded? Read this section to explore how our communication about subjects such as religion can make employees feel included or excluded and how this affects their engagement and retention.

Religion is one of those topics, like money and politics, that we believe should never be discussed at work. Perhaps the problem isn't the topic of religion itself but our lack of comfort and skill in having meaningful, respectful conversations. Many people feel strongly about their religious beliefs, and therefore it may be more natural to advocate one's own views than to inquire about those of others. Often, too, conversations about politics can lead to careless comments about religion, damaging trust and respect among staff.

This section is not about the legalities of talking about religion at work. It's about digging deeper into how our *communication about religion* influences work culture and employee engagement. As a leader, whatever your personal beliefs, you have a stake in increasing employee inclusion. When employees feel a sense of belonging, they will be more engaged, productive, and loyal.

Avoid assumptions. Assumptions can lead to misunderstanding and exclusion. When we assume that others share our religious beliefs, those who do not may feel excluded from the team—although many people will not come out and tell you that. Employees belong to many different religions and denominations, or they may not identify as religious at all. According to the Pew Research Center (2015), about one-quarter of U.S. citizens have no religious affiliation: They may be agnostic, atheist, or adhere to no particular religion. A leader in an environment historically marked by a lack of diversity may be prone to making unhelpful assumptions about employees.

Look and listen. What religious or spiritual messages are present in your work environment? Does the lunch table conversation touch on church or temple or a particular religious organization's activities? Are people encouraged to pray for others? Does your workplace acknowledge and accommodate some religious holidays but not others? Ask yourself, "Could some people feel excluded by these kinds of conversations?" If so, take the lead in encouraging more open and inclusive conversations.

Be who you are. The very idea that we should take care in how we discuss our religious beliefs at work runs the risk of being dismissed as being about political correctness—but it is not about that, or about having to silence your spiritual self. It is about considering the impact of your words and actions on employees whose work you respect and value. You set a tone as a leader, and you can be both authentic and inclusive. For example, if you are Christian and speaking about your religion, use "I" instead of "we." It's a small change, but if an employee is not part of the "we," your comments may make them feel excluded or judged negatively.

The same goes for religiously affiliated organizations. Although faith-based institutions can be expected to proclaim that faith, they often need to hire people of other religions or no religion to carry out the organization's work. Employees need not share the same religious beliefs to respect and carry out the organization's mission. When it comes to leading people, behavior is what people are accountable for, not their personal religious beliefs.

Be respectfully curious. When you talk with employees who have religious traditions that are different from your own, look for an opportunity to learn more those traditions. For example, you could say, "I'm not familiar with those traditions; could you tell me about them?" Don't look to any individual to speak on behalf of a particular religion. Rather, show interest and respect as you learn more about diverse customs and ideas—another key to employee engagement.

Examine your workplace policies. Review your policies against the Tanenbaum Diversity Checklist (2020). Start a conversation with other leaders about ways to create an open, respectful culture in which all employees feel included. When it comes to celebrations, dietary requirements, diversity education, and so on, solicit input from staff and make sure everyone has an equal opportunity to share their ideas. Tanenbaum also encourages developing an "accommodation mind-set" to describe thinking about diversity in a way that creates a welcoming and inclusive culture.

2. INTRODUCTED LEADERS

> **Are you more of an introvert than an extrovert?** Introversion, like extroversion, influences your leadership approach. This section suggests ways to nurture your introvert self and to prevent misunderstandings when you are communicating with people who are more extroverted.

Myth: Extroverts make better leaders. Reality: Both strong and weak leaders can be found in *any* personality style. Another truth is that personality traits are not the same as skill. Informed by the work of Myers and Briggs and their widely used Myers-Briggs Type Indicator (www.myersbriggs.org/), this section will help you identify your personality type and understand how it impacts your leadership.

You might be introverted if you:

- Prefer thinking things through before speaking versus thinking out loud
- Feel drained of energy in high-stimulus situations
- Feel more energized working alone or with a small group than in an open team setting

No one is "purely" one personality style or another—introvert or extrovert. We are all made up of a complex array of traits, and personality type is not static like blood type. But when it comes to navigating the energy dynamic of our internal and external worlds, most people lean more in one direction than the other.

Stereotypes of extroverted leaders as charismatic and outwardly verbal can make it tough for introverts to get noticed for leadership opportunities. It's a little like the extroverted kids in the classroom who raise their hand with their whole body, drawing all the attention, while leaving the more deliberate and internally focused introverted students unnoticed.

When it comes to being a leader, you have to be you. Being authentically you starts with spending time reflecting on who you are. Exploring your personality type is a fun and useful way to be positively self-centered. If you are an introvert:

Don't assume you won't be a great public speaker. Susan Cain, a strong introvert, is an example to the contrary. Her TED talk "The Power of Introverts" (Cain 2012) has garnered more than 25 million views! Effective speaking takes practice, and anyone who wants to excel must do the drills. Most of my best speaking ideas have come from a colleague who is extremely introverted and a gifted speaker and educator. She is passionate about her content and uses creative techniques to engage her audience in learning—proof that introversion is not the same as talent. Nor is introversion the same as shyness. Introversion is about how you reenergize. After teaching all day, my colleague seeks time alone. Because I understand our personality differences, I don't take that personally, which is a huge benefit in our working relationship!

Be conscious of your facial expressions. A common experience among introverts is that people often ask them, "Are you mad at me?" The introvert's thinking face may look a lot like irritation or anger. Be aware that you may *feel* approachable, but others may not experience you as such. Although we may think that others should assume our good intent, we are still accountable for the messages we are sending out.

Be mindful of the toll that "peopling" takes on you. The best use of personality tools is understanding how you are wired so that you can meet your needs. We all need to know what kind of fuel our engine requires to run, and then it's up to us to go after it. Manage your energy using these techniques:

- Allowing—and valuing as productive—the thinking time you need before beginning a new task or project

- Asking for agendas and written materials to review prior to meetings
- Seeking out opportunities to work alone
- Requesting time to think about or process others' questions before responding

Reveal your thinking. Help others understand your personality and what makes you tick. People want to know what you think, but when they don't, they will make things up. This is not helpful. Develop a habit of regularly asking yourself, "Who might benefit from knowing what is on my mind?"

Skeptical of personality instruments? Be open to asking, "What can I learn from personality assessments that can make me a better leader?" With an open mind, these tools (there are many!) can help individuals and teams appreciate, rather than fight, diverse approaches to work and life.

3. WHO WE DON'T SEE

Look at your inner circle of colleagues and friends—do they look more like you than not? We tend not to notice what we are used to. This section nudges you to step out of your comfort zone and into diversity conversations and helps you become a leader in building a culture of respect.

Years ago while I was facilitating a discussion among elementary school students on the topic of substance abuse, the teacher pulled me aside and reminded me to allow some of the girls to speak up. Apparently, boys raise their hands quicker and higher (Sadker, Sadker, and Zittleman 2009), and I had been calling on them 100 percent of the time. I felt terrible. I hadn't even noticed I was doing this.

I had a similar "aha" moment when I was working with a group of nursing leaders, sharing our top 10 leadership books. Someone pointed out that all the books we were listing were written by white men. (This book hadn't been written yet.) My response to this was, "Well, that &*%^$es me off." Don't get me wrong, I'm not angry at white men for writing great books. I am irritated at myself that, again, I didn't notice.

We can become immune to what we are accustomed to. Noticing is a cornerstone of moving forward in respecting diversity.

As leaders, who and what we don't notice leaves people out, creates barriers, and keeps people down. We all have biases, which often operate on an unconscious level. If you shut down a little when you hear the words "diversity" and "equality" because they have come to signify things you *should* pay attention to or are required to address in hiring or staff education, or even if you believe that you do pay attention, stick with this. Diversity competence goes far beyond compliance. Effective leaders engage multiple perspectives to reach the best decisions for the customer, the organization, and the communities they serve.

Often, we are afraid to talk about diversity and equality. We don't know what to say or ask without being offensive, sounding stupid, or making others angry and defensive. How can we talk about diversity if we aren't even aware of it?

Derald Wing Sue, the author of *Microaggressions in Everyday Life: Race, Gender, and Sexual Orientation* (2010, 20) and *Overcoming our Racism: The Journey to Liberation* (2003, 65), suggests that we "make the invisible visible" and open up our thinking and action on this topic. Wing Sue makes several recommendations in his extensive writing on this subject about how we can learn to see our biases. Boiled down to a few of his actionable suggestions, consider the following:

- **Look your biases and fears in the face.** Ask yourself regularly, what do I take for granted because of my race, gender, religion, ethnicity, age, or ability? How might someone different from me perceive this? Where do I assume others see things the same way I do? Maybe they don't.

- **Look around you, and then look more broadly.** Rural Wisconsin, where I live and work, is nearly 90 percent white. This doesn't let us off the hook. There are many kinds of diversity. Family structures, beliefs, values, physical abilities, and even rural or urban are all things that people have biases about. Examine your biases. Strike up a conversation with someone who sees the world very differently than you and find at least three things you have in common. Take it upon yourself to learn—there are many resources.

- **Assume you probably have hurt someone and be willing to talk about it.** Like me, you may have done or said things not knowing you were being hurtful or excluding someone. Talk about it. Open up a dialogue about it with other leaders. Discuss with your leadership team opportunities for improvement in communicating to include everyone. Ask for feedback from staff about how your messages are received. In my workshop evaluations, I have added a question" "Did the presenter treat all participants with respect?" It offers the opportunity for feedback that I can use to grow and learn. How might you modify a question like this for your own use?

- **Be courageous. Stand up and speak up.** When others speak in ways that exclude or belittle others, speak up. Consider your own comments about politics, religion, race, or (fill in the blank). You have an opportunity as a leader to broaden others' thinking. This is not about being careful with what you say; it is about caring. Start by saying, "I'm not comfortable with that comment. Can we talk about it?"

4. PAUSE YOUR BIAS

Do you have biases? Of course you do—we all do. Biases are learned from an early age. As a leader, how do you become aware of your biases so that you remain open to diverse perspectives? This section shares a model for pausing your biases and offers prompts for reflecting on the origins of your biases.

Imagine being sick and lying in a hospital bed. Now picture a nurse coming in to take your vital signs and care for you.

Was the nurse you pictured male or female? It's likely that your mental image of a nurse was female—a simple example of how bias operates in our minds. In fact, about 90 percent of U.S. nurses are female (U.S. Census Bureau 2013), so that bias might not be surprising. Experience and culture are two sources of bias development. However, biases stay with us even after facts change. This would have been evident if I had asked you to imagine a doctor. Many of us would have pictured a male doctor, even though in 2017 there were more female than male medical students enrolled in the United States (Heiser 2017).

This example pertained to gender bias, but biases are evident everywhere. Often, they operate unconsciously and affect our daily interactions and decisions.

Why bother to look at our unconscious biases, if consciously we believe in fairness? As a leader, biases can make a difference in how you act in interviewing, hiring, delegation assignments, deference, pay, and so on. Bias is not always negative. Sometimes it operates in a way that intends to be helpful but actually robs others of opportunity.

Rollo May (1994, 100), a psychologist and author, said that "freedom is the capacity to pause between stimulus and response."

Think about this: You see or hear something, and before your brain reacts, you hit "pause." During that pause, we have a moment to choose more wisely what we say or do.

Howard Ross (2014), a recognized leader in addressing bias, suggests developing a mental habit to PAUSE in situations in which bias may arise. Using the earlier nursing example, we can apply Ross's model:

> **P—Pay attention** to the thought process behind your initial judgments (e.g., a male nurse doesn't seem natural; men are not nurturing; men should be tough, not tender).
>
> **A—Acknowledge** your reactions and feelings (e.g., I feel uncomfortable with the idea of a male nurse because it is unfamiliar or doesn't fit with my mental image of a nurse).
>
> **U—Understand** that there may be other reactions to consider (e.g., men can bring many strengths to nursing; anyone can want to help others heal).
>
> **S—Select** the response that is most empowering (e.g., I can see male nurses as those who want to heal others).
>
> **E—Execute** (e.g., I treat male nurses with respect).

We do so many things on autopilot just to get through the day. It would be impossible to notice everything that approaches our senses all day long. But this habit of quick assessments and reactions can leave us blind to the biases we all have that get in the way of treating people fairly. To reduce bias, we must develop awareness. How can we train ourselves to do this? By applying and developing a practice of critical thinking.

- **Start by assuming that you are biased.** As they say in addiction treatment, you have to admit to a problem before recovery can begin. Until you acknowledge that bias exists, it's hard to take your awareness to the next level. Decide to become aware of your biases. If it is important to you to be able to say "I am a fair and equitable leader," being willing to admit to the biases that operate under your radar is the first step toward making that statement true.

- **Take note.** How strongly do you feel about the situation? Take the nursing example: If your reaction was slightly surprised but unemotional—"That's true, it could be a male nurse"—you are more likely to be open to fairness in the future. If your reaction was stronger—"OK, but a male nurse would be very weird"—you might have a barrier to fairness. When that happens,

- **Seek evidence.** What evidence might you consider to learn more? Examine facts and avoid seeking opinions that confirm what you already believe (this is another form of bias, called confirmation bias). Using our nursing example, can you find any data showing that male nurses have better, similar, or worse patient outcomes or job performance? Beware of single or limited incidence "data": For example, knowing one male nurse with a poor bedside manner isn't sufficient evidence that men cannot be nurturing and therefore good at nursing. If you've known one male nurse, you've known one male nurse—not the entire population of men in nursing.

- **It's OK to be uncertain.** One reason we have biases is to put the world into neat, easily understandable categories. The world rarely cooperates with this illusion. Anytime you are sure of something, it's a good time to ask yourself critical questions about what biases have led you to think a certain way.

5. MANAGING AND BEING MANAGED BY MILLENNIALS

Have you experienced generational conflicts as millennials have begun to change the culture of the workplace? Every generation has different priorities and ways of working. This section shares tips for adapting to the changing workforce and building a generationally mixed team.

As a child, when I complained about getting up early to get on the school bus, my dad would say, "When *I* was a kid we had to *walk five miles* to school, and it was uphill both ways!" It seems that every generation wants the next one to pay their dues. My generation of baby boomers (born 1946–64) did this to Generation X (born 1965–80) when they bumped into us in the workplace. (The next section talks more about Gen X.) Millennials face both baby boomers and Gen Xers as two well-established forces in the workplace—and this is not always an easy mix. The media has made much of the ways in which millennials—those born between 1980 and 1995, also known as Generation Y—are turning the workplace upside down (Espinoza, Ukleja, and Rusch 2010).

The number-one complaint I hear about millennials (I am not proud to admit I have said it myself) is that they seem "entitled." But doesn't every generation want better for the next one? The parents of these millennials *created* their expectations with regular reminders reinforcing that they could do anything they set their minds to. It makes sense that millennials believe it—and truly, I want them to believe it. What might seem like entitlement might just be expectations of greatness. Is it so bad for young people to expect great things? Those of us in older generations need them to be great. We need millennials to harness their knowledge and their numbers—which now surpass the record number of boomers, according to U.S. Census Bureau estimates—to lead us through the challenges now and into the future.

Conflicts arise, however, when generational cohorts view workplace norms differently and believe their own view is the way it "ought" to be. This stance is unhelpful in resolving conflicts. This is a place for the coaching question introduced in chapter 1, "Do you want to be right, or do you want to be effective?"

The following tips will help you work effectively with millennial employees:

- **Develop a relationship with younger employees.** Millennials may not be loyal to their employer the way previous generations were, but a real relationship with a manager is critical to making employees feel connected. Spend time getting to know millennials and what makes them tick.

- **Show younger employees how their work is helping them advance in the organization.** This means having conversations regularly about their work, why it matters, how it can help them grow.

- **Give more frequent feedback, face-to-face.** Yearly performance evaluations won't cut it. This mentoring and feedback are part of your job as a leader, not work in addition to your job.

- **Create benchmarks for progress.** Handhold more with what the expectations are, and reinforce progress.

- **When there are no opportunities for advancement, look for alternative ways to switch up jobs.** Expect that if you don't, younger employees will leave for opportunities that look like advancement.

- **Teach them to be your boss!** Members of this generation are the leaders of tomorrow. Spend time mentoring them to be leaders you want to follow.

- **Leverage millennials' teamwork orientation.** How can you create team-building opportunities to keep younger employees connected?

- **Have a party on their first day of work**—not on the day they leave.
- **Keep an open mind to what millennials can teach you about technology and connection.** This generation may be less tech savvy than they are tech unafraid. We can learn from younger employees about taking risks and trying new things.
- **Hold people accountable for expectations, but also adapt.** Every generation has had an impact on the world of work, and millennials are no different. This generation is already doing amazing things, and we need them to!

6. GENERATION X—FORGOTTEN AGAIN

Do your Generation X leaders get the respect they have earned? This section reminds you of a few things you may have taken for granted that were inspired by this demographic.

After I had written in my monthly newsletter about baby boomers and millennials, a Generation X colleague copied me on this lighthearted (I think!?) note that he sent to his team:

> "Notice that the Generation X gets mentioned early in one article and then ignored after that. That's OK because we Gen Xers are used to being ignored."

Oops. He was right. Generation X (those born between 1964 and 1980) is historically a smaller demographic. Until the beginning of the baby boomers' exodus to retirement, Gen Xers were the fewest in number of any generational diversity group discussion I facilitated. Their airtime got shortchanged, squeezed between two larger groups whose more evident tensions needed to be addressed. But Gen Xers fill many leadership positions, and they have had a positive and significant impact on the workplace in many ways.

The following are some things to appreciate about Generation X:

- **Meritocracy.** Generation X pushed the notion of valuing employees for results they produce, not how early they arrive, how late they stay, their tenure, or their title. This cohort helped shift the focus in the workplace from effort to outcome—opening up time for everyone.
- **Business casual.** Thank Gen Xers for khakis, logo wear, and casual Fridays. Not everyone agrees on this, but saying goodbye to uptight clothing makes many people happier *and* more productive!
- **Early adoption of technology.** My Gen X niece advised me early on, "You can't be scared of the computer." Generation X jumped in and didn't worry about making mistakes while learning—something previous generations seemed to struggle with, perhaps because they wanted to protect their position or image. This generation paved the way for tech innovation.
- **Work-life balance (sort of).** This generation challenged the idea that family and health must be sacrificed for career success. The first part-time physician leader I ever coached was a Generation Xer. "Part-time physician" was not a term used by previous generations of physicians. Yet in the desire to have it all, I have heard many Gen Xers say that striving for balance between career goals and family and personal time is stressful. While many of us are still figuring out work-life balance, pushback on the idea that "work is king" was the right thing to do. The health and families of generations before and after Generation X will benefit from this challenge.
- **Asking why.** Because Gen Xers asked "why," we are less likely to do things just because that's the way we've always done it. They push us to keep asking, innovating, and

working toward continual improvement and efficiencies. In business, if we are not innovating, we are falling behind.

- **Increased access to leaders.** The influence of Generation X has helped flatten organizational charts, reducing the hierarchical structure. Previous generations had stricter rules about who could approach whom in the organization and imposed communication barriers between the "workers" and leadership. Because this generation was raised to be self-reliant at an early age, Gen Xers have removed boundaries in the workplace. As a result, corporate knowledge and wisdom are more accessible to everyone, which sets the stage for increased employee engagement.

Let it not be said that Generation X is forgotten. We may take these things for granted, but we owe Generation X gratitude for driving change in the workplace. We will continue to benefit from the ideas this generation brings to leadership.

7. SUPERVISING BABY BOOMERS

> **Have you ever had a battle of wills with a baby boomer who won't let go? Or, are you that baby boomer?** This section offers some considerations to help conflicting generations understand each other and move forward to a productive partnership.

Things have changed—as they do. Baby boomers have been surpassed by millennials as the largest adult generation, and by 2028, they are projected to account for a minority of the adult population. Members of Generation X, the smallest of the three demographic cohorts, are now moving into leadership roles vacated by retiring baby boomers, while millennials, the largest group, are making their voices heard. Baby boomers are likely to have supervisors who are much younger, posing challenges for both employees and managers.

To facilitate conversation between generations, I ask people to split up into groups of baby boomers, Generation X, and millennials and give each group a set of questions exploring influences on their worldview, such as technology, parenting styles, cultural markers, and so on. I follow up this small group work with a large group dialogue whose purpose is to improve working partnerships through increased understanding of differences and similarities. Two interesting observations always surface.

First, the millennial group is always done first. I have no way of scientifically explaining this phenomenon, but I often wonder whether, in my baby boomer love for meeting and talking and processing, if I have failed to make the exercise meaningful before asking them to do it. Have I neglected to connect the dots between the exercise and its value before we started? Could I have made it more fun?

Second, I always have to cut off the baby boomers. Yes, there is more history to cover, but this may also reflect a cohort of people who are very attached to their worldviews. It makes sense that a group that has been in control and that has shaped the current work climate might find it difficult to let go of that control.

Here are some notes for baby boomer employees:

- Reflect on your need for control. What would happen if you allowed yourself to be challenged—not on something you are already poised to give up, but on something (a process or way of working) that you hold near and dear? What could you learn from letting go?

- You may have more years of experience, but learning is a two-way street. Remind yourself often that younger leaders have much to teach you. They can nudge you to see things a different way and to find new—and often quicker and better—solutions.

- Allow your millennial coworkers to give you permission to have a little fun at work.

Here are some notes for millennial leaders:

- Explore why baby boomers are so attached to their way of doing things. Ask gently, but ask.
- Be patient, even if they stumble at first. Your questions will make them think. Make sure you are approachable when they are ready to talk.
- You give up nothing, and stand to gain a strong ally, if you let your baby boomer employees know that you value and want to learn from their experience. Bring it up openly, but . . .
- Don't apologize for being in a leadership role. You've got this.

What is revealed through these conversations is not the differences between generations, but the similarities. Employees and leaders of all age groups can agree that they want to be:

- Respected and treated as an equal professional
- Involved in the decisions that impact them
- Honored for their expertise, training, education, experience
- Listened to
- In a positive professional relationship with their manager
- Treated as a person, not as a stereotype.

The last item is the bottom line when it comes to any kind of diversity. When you supervise someone, understand many diversities broadly, but treat each person as a unique individual. Don't assume anything. Ask—and listen for—how they learn, what kind of feedback helps them succeed, what they know, and what they need from you.

CHAPTER 9

Teamwork

FEW WORK OUTCOMES rely on solo operations. We get things done by people working together. When our teams function like well-oiled machines, efficiency and productivity are the result. This chapter explores what is needed to make teamwork happen.

SELF-ASSESSMENT SCORING:

1—I am struggling with or not yet skilled at this.

2—I am starting to work on improving at this, but I need more skill building.

3—I am making some consistent progress in improving at this.

4—I am doing very well in this area.

Determine your current level of skill on these teamwork competencies (score 1–4):

1. I create a safe environment for my teams to engage productively; everyone contributes to the work. Score: _____

2. I know when I need to act independently and when I need to bring in stakeholders, and that decision is reflected in my behaviors and actions. Score: _____

3. I use effective methods to facilitate a sense of ownership of the organization among employees. Score: _____

4. I proactively manage the challenges that arise when I inherit a team I did not select. Score: _____

Now explore the corresponding sections that follow to learn how to improve skills that need work or enhance your current skills.

1. WHAT MAKES A TEAM PRODUCTIVE?

How can you encourage more balanced contributions from team members? This section will prompt you to consider the ways that your actions influence others' participation. It also explores how you can make it safe for team members to participate more.

You've participated in work teams and have ideas about what makes a team productive. Google studied the effectiveness of its teams and found that teamwork boils down to two consistent qualities that, as a leader, you can influence directly (Duhigg 2016):

- Everyone has a chance to have their say and be heard—a skill known as conversational turn-taking.
- The team environment is psychologically safe—the skill of empathy, or having the sensitivity to read others.

Making even small improvements in these areas is worth considering.

Consider the following to encourage conversational turn-taking:

- **Do you talk too much?** Leaders often get the floor more because of their role, and it becomes easy to dominate the conversation. Set a task for yourself to ask what others think at specified intervals—use a timer if you need a reminder. Try these prompts:
  - I have shared my thoughts. What do others think?
  - Poke some holes in my plan and tell me how you see it differently.
  - Am I missing something in my conclusions? I'd like everyone to throw out alternate stances for us all to consider.

  Once others are invited to give input, listen with interest.

Not sure if you talk too much? Ask someone you trust, "How much of the speaking time am I using in this meeting?" Or, "In the next meeting, I'd like you to just track how many times I interrupt when someone else is talking." Feedback is your friend. Thank that person.

Do you allow someone else to talk too much? Even a smart and articulate team member can dominate the conversation, shutting down others and causing team engagement to suffer. Address the behavior for the good of the team and for the individual's success. You don't want people to groan about them, even if only inwardly. Feedback is their friend, too.

Consider the following to make the team environment feel safe:

Get good at reading others. Can you perceive the meaning behind what others say even when they aren't using their words? An interesting and fun way to explore this is to take the "Reading the Eyes in the Mind" test (Baron-Cohen 2020). Work to improve your score by paying more attention to nonverbal cues and the ways faces convey information. Don't jump to conclusions, but instead:

- Observe. Look up, consider facial expressions, and contemplate whether they match the tone of voice.
- Make a guess, then ask about what you notice. For example, "Your facial expression makes me wonder whether you are puzzled; is that right? Can you tell me more about that?"

Decide that safety matters. You have to believe that safety matters before you can work on it. It may be easy to dismiss psychological safety as "their problem, not mine." If the cost of speaking up is too high, though, it becomes your problem. People will hold back on ideas, safety concerns, and creativity for fear of being wrong or being ridiculed. Create a culture in which people can speak up, disagree without losing status, learn from their mistakes, and laugh a little. Leaders—you go first.

2. INDEPENDENT CUSSES AND TEAM TENDERS

Are you an independent-minded leader? Do you sometimes get into trouble because you forge ahead without involving others? Alternatively, are you the one who routinely asks who else needs to be at the worktable? This section explores how our group or individual orientation plays a part in our approach to work. Learn about safeguards that you can put in place if you prefer to work more like a lone wolf than in a pack.

For as much as I write and teach others about the importance of team building and working collaboratively, I admit to two truths:

- Being a team player does not come naturally to me.
- I keep working at it, and it is not easy.

Personality traits explain a lot. "Independent cusses" were born with an independent streak, taking ideas to action with a single-mindedness that works (when it works!). It's not a derogatory term. Those with this independent trait can achieve great things through their singular focus. Think of this trait as the zoom lens of a camera.

"Team tenders" are born with a predisposition to look at things from a group perspective rather than an individual perspective. They naturally add a step between "ideas" and "action," and that step is to involve others. Think of this trait as the wide angle lens of a camera.

In healthcare and many other industries, little can be done alone, because all the parts are interconnected for the benefit of the patient or customer. Independent cusses have big ideas and get results, but they need team tenders to keep everyone on track and working together. Regardless of your personality preferences, you are responsible for working effectively with others.

- **Team tenders, speak up.** When you have been left out of planning, information loops, decisions, and so on, speak up! Approach your more independent-minded colleagues assuming good intent—because most of the time, that is the case. They think differently than you do, and they need your perspective.
- **Independent cusses, develop a habit of checking in with key team members.** Ask, "How am I doing at keeping you informed?" Give a brief rundown of progress on projects you are working on. Share the what, why, and how of your

project. Ask, "Can you think of anything in your work or goals that intersects with what I am doing that I should consider?" To take this to the next level.

- **Do a stakeholder analysis.** Project management tools help prevent miscommunication. They force you to identify up front the people who have a stake in the outcome or impact of your project. You've probably already thought about the obvious stakeholders, but the less obvious ones are likely to be missed. Independent cusses, sit down with your more systems-thinking colleagues and brainstorm who will be directly or indirectly impacted by your work throughout the project.

- **Before hitting send, consider "reply all."** An independent cuss will cuss when someone hits "reply all" and they don't see a need for it. In turn, team tenders will feel left out and undervalued when others do not "reply all." If you tend toward undercommunicating, ask yourself regularly, "Who else might want to know about this, or who might construe not being included as a slight?" For those of you who are more likely to reply all, pause to consider whether you are using this function judiciously. Avoid overloading inboxes with nonessential content to reduce the risk that your important messages will be overlooked.

- **Listen to how often you say "I" instead of "we."** You may not change a thing, but pay attention to your words to understand what they reveal about your connection to your team and the way you work. At the same time. . . .

- **Appreciate your "I."** Not everything is done by a team. Individual contributions are important, too. There is no one right way to get work done, and we do our best when we bring our natural talents to the table. The trick is remembering that any trait that is overused can become a problem.

- **Offer to help out with team efforts when you normally would not get involved.** For example, if you don't like or see the need for work parties, go anyway and help with the cleanup.
- **Do a personality inventory with your team.** All team members can benefit from the insights into themselves and others that personality inventories provide and learn to appreciate the gifts that each team member brings. Inventories are a fun way to explore areas in which we are challenged. They can teach us not to take these differences personally by providing an objective platform for communication about those differences.

3. WE

Do you want to see more engagement from your team? If you have it, people will refer to their employer as "we" rather than "they." This section offers suggestions for encouraging ownership in your organizational culture.

We, not *they*. Which word do your employees use when speaking about your organization? "*We* are offering a new service here at *our* hospital" has a much different tone than "Sounds like *they* are going to start a new service at *the* hospital." The former has a ring of pride, the latter, mild curiosity at best.

We says:

- I belong.
- My voice matters.
- I'm committed and engaged in my work—I'm "all in."

They sounds a little more tentative. It implies:

- I work here, this is my job but I could just as easily work somewhere else.

Employee engagement is critical to organizational success. How can we motivate employees to think in terms of *we*, not *they*?

Increase autonomy. Engagement goes up when we stop overmanaging employees. Some jobs don't have much flexibility, but think about where you *could* give up some control and let employees decide? In his book *Drive: The Surprising Truth About What Motivates Us* (2009, 105), Daniel Pink describes four specific ways that we can offer autonomy:

- **Time**—Can you give the employee freedom to decide *when* something is done?
- **Task**—Can team members decide for themselves in some situations *what* tasks they will do to make the most of their strengths?
- **Team**—Are there opportunities for people to choose *with whom* they work?
- **Technique**—Even if you define the final outcome, is there a way to give employees a choice of *how* to get there?

Keep the toolbox full. When assigning work, make sure to ask employees whether they have the materials, resources, tools, and access to the information they need. Establish a reputation as a leader who will find the resources employees need to do their work.

Watch your language. How do *you* talk about your organization or about senior leaders? It matters. If you find yourself saying *they*, what does that mean about your level of engagement? It may be that the environment is not as engaging as it could be. It might also mean that you could do something to change the environment. How can you speak with your leaders to increase your own engagement?

De-jargonize yourself. Watch out for the use of job-specific lingo. Jargon implies the existence of an in-group (those who know what the lingo means) and an out-group (those who don't). You run the risk of excluding and disengaging those who don't know the lingo and don't feel comfortable asking.

Give stuff away. Share what you know and delegate the fun assignments. If something works for you and someone shows an interest, give them the opportunity to try it or learn it. Tell people your secrets of success and help them try it, too.

Think about other departments. For broader organizational engagement, what could you do to shine a light on other departments? Consider departments that you rarely think about. Where does your work intersect? What opportunities can you take advantage of to thank, recognize, or speak well of other departments and the work they contribute to your organization's success? Do they need an invitation to collaborate to feel more connected to and valued by your department?

Call people by name. Do you know and use the name of the person who checks you out in the cafeteria line? The person who cleans your office? Nothing is as validating to someone as saying their name when you greet them. Everyone matters.

Talk about the why. *Why* does it matter that I do this report, fill out this form, or finish this project? Explain the reason behind the tasks so that people feel a sense of purpose rather than merely crossing tasks off their list.

4. INHERITING A TEAM

Have you become the leader of a team that someone else selected? This section offers insights into the challenges of working with a team you didn't choose and outlines the steps you can take to set the right tone going forward.

Most promotions to management roles come with a honeymoon phase of excitement, but the glow fades quickly when you realize that the team you inherited is not exactly the team you would have chosen. These are some of the specific challenges you may face:

- The team may have been without a manager for some time and doesn't think it needs one now either, "thanks anyway!"
- One or more team members applied for your job and did not get it.
- One of the team members used to be in your position. They may have stepped down from management responsibilities but still have a lot of influence with the team and may not always support your vision.
- You have big ideas for growth and improvement, but the team sees no downside to the status quo and no upside to change.
- The previous manager was beloved, and changing anything feels like you are criticizing that person.
- The team members are old enough to be your parents or even grandparents, and it is a daily challenge to be taken seriously.

First, know that these are challenges you can face and address successfully, and you are not alone. Take a deep breath and remember that you were chosen for this role. Leading takes courage, so take heart! Whether you are just getting started with your new team or you want a fresh start, build your confidence and allow your team to see your leadership come through as you consider the following approaches:

Apologize for mistakes but not for your existence. Reframe your thinking about guilt, especially when it comes to asking others to do things: "We are at work to work, so why would I need to apologize or feel guilty for asking people to do work?"

Ask the team for help. You can't achieve your department's goals without the team's help, so ask for it. "I need your help to make this happen. Can I count on you to _____?" Be specific so the team members have the opportunity to be specific in their commitment, which helps you with accountability later.

Be bold and clear about your vision. Create a focal point for the future where team members want to go. It will help guide your actions. Are today's actions helping you get there? If yes, great. Reinforce. If no, partner with the team to explore what corrections or actions will help you achieve your vision.

Write and share your "owner's manual." Create a simple questionnaire for all of your team members to fill out and share among themselves. Include opportunities for people to respond to items such as, "Here are some things to know about my personality, my hot buttons, what works best in communicating with me, how I like to structure my day, my non-negotiables, etc."

Write a paragraph envisioning how you want to be thought of in ten years. Use this document to guide your behavior, composure, and attitude today. Post it where you can see it, or create a reminder text or email to send it to yourself. Ask a mentor to check in with you periodically to see whether you are adhering to it. Taking the long view in leadership will help during tough times in the short run.

Address the elephant in the room, and then move on. The "elephant" may be a difference in age or experience between you and your team, or it may be that a team member wanted your job but didn't get it. Remember empathy first. Put yourself in their place and acknowledge how they feel. Begin with, "I want this to work for both of us. What can we do to move our relationship to a better place?" We can't demand that anyone move on from their feelings, but when we truly listen and make time for meaningful dialogue, we *allow* them to move on. There is a big difference.

Remember that resistance to change is almost always about fear. Share the sense of urgency (the why) for the change. Find a way to show what is in it for the team. Reassure team members that you will provide the resources to help them succeed in the new way, and then do so.

Give it time. View your frustration as a symptom instead of a driver. If you find yourself feeling frustrated, ask yourself this question: "What am I taking personally that is not about me?"

Change your team members if you need to. This approach is the last one for a reason. A whole new workforce team is not waiting for anyone these days. Coach the people you have to help them grow. It is an investment worth making! But if team members cannot or will not go in the direction you are leading them, keeping them may be detrimental to the team and will reflect poorly on you if you allow underperformance or undermining. Prepare by getting coaching yourself so that you are ready for this tough conversation.

CHAPTER 10

Culture

CULTURE RULES, AND LEADERS play a huge role in creating, maintaining, and supporting it. Even when we know that culture is important, we still might question how to influence it. My best advice? Just start.

SELF-ASSESSMENT SCORING:

1—I am struggling with or not yet skilled at this.

2—I am starting to work on improving at this, but I need more skill building.

3—I am making some consistent progress in improving at this.

4—I am doing very well in this area.

Determine your current level of skill on these culture competencies (score 1–4):

1. I am aware of my impact in shaping the workplace culture and use strategies to keep moving in the right direction. Score: _____

2. I have an employee retention strategy that is working to keep good people and prevent turnover. Score: _____

3. I am aware of the markers of good morale. I use multiple techniques to engage employees in improving and maintaining positive morale. Score: _____

4. I follow a communication plan when an employee departs from the organization that leads to a positive outcome. Score: _____

5. I avoid blaming myself or others when things go wrong, and I understand the high costs of blame in organizational life. Score: _____

Now explore the corresponding sections that follow to learn how to improve skills that need work or enhance your current skills.

1. CULTURE RULES

Are you working on improving your workplace culture? "Culture" can seem a bit mysterious. This section offers practical steps for instigating positive change in organizational culture.

The best leaders confirm that culture matters, and many even say that it overrides strategy. But how do you make an impact as an individual on this thing called "culture"? Start by considering these two points:

- **You already are making an impact.** Just by being in a leadership role, you influence your environment. Often, leaders underestimate their influence. Everything you say and do—your words, your body language, your written communications—shape the organization's culture more than you might realize. What kinds of messages are you already sending?

- **Culture is formed "one handshake at a time."** You can't shake hands with a culture, but you can shake hands (or bow or bump elbows) with individuals. Those individual connections, making "deposits" over time, can mobilize the team and help you avoid the pitfalls of low morale, undermining, and poor engagement.

The following ideas can make a big difference in creating a thriving, engaged, and desirable work culture:

Eat lunch with different people. Push yourself to eat lunch or take coffee breaks with different people from different departments on a regular basis. This is a simple way to break down silos. You might have to invite yourself to join a group of employees who always eat together, but when you do, you make yourself more approachable. Later, when a problem comes up, they will feel more comfortable coming to you to discuss it. That creates a much more desirable culture than one in which people grumble among themselves.

Become known for a phrase that you can live by. Your catchphrase will become a part of the organizational culture. One of my managers early in my career regularly used a phrase that still pops into my head when I face a difficult conversation. After coaching me on a sticky employee issue, he walked me to the door and said, "Remember, be courageous." He was creating a courageous culture (as well as creating a lasting reminder in my brain). What is your phrase?

Be the first to accept a challenge. One healthcare system CEO supported both his employees and the local community by sponsoring health club memberships for all hospital employees as part of a wellness initiative. He was among the first to do the heavy lifting of exercising, losing weight, and getting fit. When you ask others to make a higher commitment, walking the talk speaks volumes.

Interview new hires. After their first few weeks on the job, ask them what they notice about the culture, both positive and negative. You might be surprised what new eyes see in the environment.

Describe your ideal culture. We might think we know what kind of culture we're striving for, but building an organizational culture is kind of like car shopping when your only criterion is that you need a new car. You may end up with something you don't want. Grab a flip chart and markers, meet with your team, ask and record their answers to the following questions:

- "How would you describe the ideal workplace culture?"
- "How would you describe our current workplace culture?" (Or use employee opinion survey results as a starting point)
- "As we look at the current and the ideal cultures we've described, what are your ideas for getting from where we are to where we want to be?"

Brainstorm ideas and facilitate a discussion to prioritize one or two ideas that will yield the most impact and produce some quick wins.

Delegate, don't abdicate. It's tempting to surrender your authority when a responsibility is uncomfortable (e.g., you hate scheduling conflicts). However, that vacuum creates an opportunity for a negative subculture to develop and for others to usurp your authority, creating staff power struggles just off your radar. Delegating properly keeps the accountability with you while sharing the workload.

Here are some additional culture improvement strategies that I think are worth making explicit:

- Genuinely say "good morning" to everyone.
- Hold people accountable to a high standard while forgiving honest mistakes.
- Give short speeches.
- Demonstrate and speak about the importance of doing whatever it takes to serve the customer.
- Make a habit of speaking about what you are learning, and invite others to do so as well.
- Take an interest in people: "That sounds interesting—tell me more."
- Never gossip. Period.
- Thank people, and create venues for people to thank each other or share what is going well.
- Explain *why* you are doing what you are doing.
- Address cultural underperformers, particularly leaders who report to you.
- Turn complaints about other departments into problem-solving discussions.
- Hire for the culture you want to create. Specifically, ask behavior-based questions in interviews to understand how the candidate has demonstrated in the past the behavior that fits your environment. Train your team and include them in team-based interviews and structured selection processes that prioritize cultural fit.

2. PREVENTING THE HIGH COST OF TURNOVER

> **Are you experiencing more staff turnover than you'd like? Are you thinking about how to retain the team you have?** This section focuses on how you engage employees to commit to the organization and stay with it. It offers actions that you can take right away and others that you can use to build a long-term retention strategy.

No one wants to come to work and feel as if they don't know what they are doing or where they belong. It's easy to forget how difficult the first few months on the job are. Nurses make up a large part of the healthcare workforce, and we have learned a lot about retention by studying them. Their longevity has been shown to be strongly linked to feelings of competence, support, and sense of belonging. Nurse residency programs (yearlong workshops, coaching, structured mentoring) that offer nurses a supportive learning course for their first year of practice demonstrate amazing results in improving retention. In a pilot project conducted with Marquette University, Wisconsin hospitals that fully supported new nurses in this residency program nearly doubled the retention rate for new hires in the first two years of practice. Some went from 50% to more than 90% retention (Bratt 2009).

Residency programs come with a cost, but what does it cost to replace an employee who leaves the organization? Estimates in the nursing literature suggest that the cost of losing an employee is nearly as high as that employee's annual salary! (Bratt 2009). Consider these costs:

- Downtime in functions when a position is not filled
- Time needed for a new hire to become competent and lost productivity during that time
- Specialty training when you lose a highly skilled employee

- Temp pay (typically at premium rates) for coverage while you are filling a position
- Overtime pay for others who are covering the open position
- Poor morale among those who are left to do the work (and the risk that they, too, will leave)
- Pileup of management and leadership duties, and the accompanying cost of stress to you, as you cover frontline work

It pays to invest in strong onboarding, which more than offsets the costs of losing employees. Efforts to increase retention are worth every penny.

How do you get people to stay? Retention starts before you even place an ad. But once you have selected the best candidate:

Build belonging. Attend to this right away. Belonging creates fertile ground for learning: We learn best when we know where we fit. Here are some of the best ideas for building belonging from those who have succeeded at it:

- Meet with new hires before they start work.
- Plan a social activity with the team outside of work.
- Greet new hires at the door on their first day.
- Give new hires a questionnaire about their favorite foods and offer some of them on day one.
- Have different staff members take the new hire to lunch or coffee each day for a week.
- Conduct a team icebreaker before tackling a project.

Build quarterly connections. Put quarterly discussions on your calendar and your new employee's. Make these discussions intentional, beyond "How are things going?" Here are some starters:

- "You've been here for three months. What is the most surprising thing you have learned so far?"

- "If you were starting today, what would you suggest that we tell you that we neglected to tell you on day one?
- "You have been here for six months. Is there anyone who has been particularly helpful to you or made you feel comfortable here?" (Learn about the employee's sense of belonging and be sure to recognize those who are named)
- "What would make you want to stay in this job a year from now? What would make you not want to stay?"

Build engagement rather than "complete orientation." Checklists have a place, but engagement is not something you can cross off a list. It is about building and maintaining relationships. Critical employee engagement factors have a direct link back to the manager:

- Giving regular actionable feedback and recognition. It must be more specific than "Great job!"
- Providing materials and tools to get the job done. Don't assume that people have what they need or know where to find it.
- Being clear about expectations. Maybe you think you have been, but you might be surprised.
- Fostering a caring environment.

Build team accountability for engagement. Make engagement a part of everyone's job, not just the manager's. Understandably, everyone wants the new person to be up to speed immediately. They've been working extra while waiting for the position to be filled. Explain to the team that if the new person is forced to sink or swim, they might sink and you'll be interviewing again. It is in everyone's best interest to take the time to teach and mentor the new team member as they build up to a reasonable workload. If you hear, "No one did that for me when I was new," learn to address this problem—which is actually a form of bullying—in the moment. Here is one possible response: "You want this person to cover for you when you need to take time off and to have your back when you are working together, so you need them to be fully competent. They need your help to get there."

Build a success plan. Clearly identify and discuss what new hires should know right away, then build in a plan so that they don't get overwhelmed by all there is to learn. Identify milestones for the job: "At three months you should be able to . . ." Repeat these milestones quarterly or even weekly, depending on the job. Make it clear that it takes time to learn how to do a job, that a learning curve is normal, and that no one can learn everything at once—things that are easy for new hires to forget.

3. WORKPLACE MORALE

Are rumblings about low morale leaving you frustrated and stressed? Read this section to explore who "owns" morale and what high morale looks and sounds like. Learn specific behaviors that leaders need to coach out of a team to support a high-morale environment.

The "beatings will continue until morale improves" method probably only works if you are a pirate. Keeping up morale can be a challenge, especially when times are tough. It is possible, but first you must assign responsibility.

Imagine securing this agreement with every staff member: "I am putting *you* in charge of our team's morale." Add it to every employee's job description and hold them accountable for it in performance reviews and employee opinion surveys. No more "It's someone else's fault."

It starts with you. Leaders ignite high morale with clear communication, reward and recognition practices, flexible work arrangements, autonomy in work styles, and fair pay and benefits. But everyone must be assigned 100 percent of the responsibility for morale for your organization to be a great place to work. What does high morale look like, and how can you nurture it?

- **Stuff gets done.** When accountability is high, morale is high. Do you set and meet important goals?
- **Employees can articulate how their work contributes to the big picture.** Are you connecting the dots between daily tasks and organizational success? Are you telling stories that highlight how important their work is to reaching the organization's goals?
- **You hear laughter.** How can you have a little more fun?
- **Colleagues volunteer and help each other.** How can you focus on building relationships between employees?
- **People freely give others credit.** Are you leading the way by recognizing others so that credit doesn't feel like a scarcity?
- **You hear people disagree respectfully.** Do you model nondefensive listening when others disagree with you? Do you foster open discussion and thoughtfully seek out and consider different views?
- **Staff show excitement about their work.** How are *you* talking about what is happening at work? Are you working on anything interesting and sharing it with others?

"People inspire you, or they drain you—pick them wisely." This statement by Hans F. Hansen, from a *Forbes* article (Bradberry 2015) on toxic people, reminds us to pay attention to the way others' energy affects us. Who are your outliers? Thank those who contribute to a welcoming workplace and manage themselves through the ups and downs of life and work. Coach those who exhibit these behaviors:

- **Don't want to come to work.** "Tell me about the last time you were excited to come to work. What kinds of things were you doing? How might you recapture some of that enthusiasm?"
- **Sigh, grumble, mutter under their breath, or don't talk at all.** "I notice heavy sighs/silence during our discussion. What is keeping you from getting more actively involved? How can you express your concerns more effectively? What impact do you think you are having on the team?"
- **Show no outward sign of disagreement.** "You don't disagree with our decisions, but I don't see you carrying them out. I need to hear the good and the bad from you; otherwise, the team's efforts suffer."
- **Spread rumors.** "The rumor mill is not to be considered a news source. If you have an issue, bring it up openly, ask me questions, and trust me to be honest with you." Earn that trustworthy reputation and then maintain it. Rumors thrive in a communication vacuum.
- **Declare themselves the spokesperson to tell you that morale sucks.** "What are you personally doing to contribute to solutions?" If they are not part of the solution, they are part of the problem. Reinforce that morale is everyone's responsibility and ask for their individual commitment to action.

One more morale destroyer that might surprise you is inconsistency among managers. When employees see other departments not being held accountable for an organization-wide standard, it undermines confidence that leadership knows what it is doing. Address inconsistencies with your leadership team and make sure all leaders are committed to remedying them before heading back to your departments.

4. DEPARTING EMPLOYEES

Have you had an employee surprise you with a resignation? If not, have you given any thought to how you would conduct yourself if that happened? It may eventually happen, and it matters how you respond in the moment and after their departure. This section will help you to prepare for this and avoid blunders that can come back to haunt you.

Employees leave the organization, whether for retirement, better opportunities for themselves or a partner elsewhere, or other reasons. The way you manage an employee's voluntary departure matters. This is not something we give a lot of thought to until it happens. Be ready to lead intentionally when employees leave and you will build trust and respect among those who stay.

> **Prepare yourself for conflicting feelings.** Too often, leaders turn sour on a well-liked employee who has the gall to leave. It is unfortunate for everyone:
>
> - **The departing employee**—who is hurt and feeling unappreciated for all they have contributed. Your high regard for them in the past appears false, and it is a kick right in the self-esteem.
> - **The remaining employees**—who empathize with the departing employee. They are asking themselves, "Can I trust that my manager really appreciates me, or is that fake, too? Do my contributions matter?"
> - **You**—when you take a departure personally, you may resent the employee for leaving you with work they won't be able to do and having to fill a position. Your employees pick up on your reactions, and it can diminish your professionalism.

Start by accepting the situation. It's OK to say that you are surprised if that is the case, but quickly move to empathy. Put yourself in the employee's shoes and congratulate them if appropriate. One way to avoid saying or asking something you'll regret is to do a lot of genuine listening. Keep the announcement brief and positive, and set a time to discuss the details of the departure. This will give you the opportunity to . . .

Take some time alone to reflect. It's alright to be angry, worried, frustrated, or whatever you feel. Deal with your emotions on your own or with your own manager or mentor. Unaddressed feelings express themselves in your tone of voice, body language, sarcasm, and so on, even if you say all the right things.

Celebrate and thank consistently. Nothing says "I'm not important" like having a going-away party for some people but not others. Obvious favoritism shows when departing employees with higher status positions, personal friendships with the boss, or long tenure get a party but employees who don't fit those descriptions do not. Talk with your team to create a way to say goodbye when someone leaves and apply it equitably. Keep in mind, too, that so many baby boomers, who were willing to wait for recognition on their way out the door, have retired. Others won't wait, and the competition is fierce for employees. When it comes to arrival and departure parties in general, focus on celebration and recognition all year around.

Stay above board on all comments about the departing employee. Continue to give credit and manage up even after the person is gone when the good work they contributed is obvious. Keep any other feelings you might have to yourself. Assume that the departing employee will stay in touch with other team members and that what you share will get back to them. This is one reason to . . .

Think of the departing employee as an advertisement for your organization. A best practice for hiring is to conduct interviews in such a way that you leave the candidate with a great feeling about your organization even if they don't get the job. They will say great things about you, and that's the best kind of marketing. When a great employee departs, treat them in a way that would make them want to come back if the opportunity presented itself. Even if they don't come back, you can influence the image they present to others about you in their new circle.

When it comes to exit interviews, it's a little too late to find out what you could have done to make a good employee stay. Make sure you are attending to employees' reasons for staying *while* they are working for you.

5. REVERSING THE HIGH COST OF BLAME

Do you tend to look for someone to blame when something goes wrong? It may seem natural to want to place blame, but most often doing so is unhelpful. This section explores the damage that blame can cause and shows how you can look for authentic accountability instead.

It's tough to admit that we are still bound by playground norms. "She started it, it's her fault!" We learn early in life to look for someone to blame to avoid punishment, and that thought process is hardwired. Some of the things we learned in kindergarten we need to unlearn—and blaming is one of them.

We might naturally outgrow blaming if it wasn't so self-reinforcing, quickly getting us off the hook and feeding our ego. It comes at a cost, though, manifesting in these ways:

- **Rework and workarounds.** Work takes longer, becomes more complicated, and is often duplicated unnecessarily when we waste time assigning blame instead of creating solutions.

- **Drama drain.** We spend hours away from our work while defending our version of a situation to get support and justify that someone else is wrong. Hours of every workday can be wasted on this drama—which means nothing else is getting done.

- **Disengaged or departing workforce.** An environment of blame reflects and breeds fear. People don't take risks in a fear-based culture. Healthcare and every other industry needs innovators. Your best and brightest will go elsewhere if the culture doesn't support trying new things even if they fail.

- **Death!** It's more permanent than getting in trouble. Problems go unreported because of the fear of blaming the messenger. Extend this to a patient who has a very bad outcome—even death—when a problem goes unreported because it was unsafe to speak up.

The flip side of blame is personal accountability. Your leadership credibility relies on accepting accountability. It is worth your time to assess your own blaming tendencies and work on letting them go. There is no sense walking through life with an unconscious fear of getting into trouble when all of us make mistakes. You are welcome to join my support group: "Hi, I am Jo Anne and I make colossal mistakes."

Today, notice your blaming thoughts. Pay careful attention to your thinking, because blaming is so ingrained that you may not even know you're doing it. Tune in the split second someone asks you for work that you haven't done, that you're unable to do, or that you've forgotten, or when things aren't turning out right. Pay attention to the temptation to blame during moments of frustration. Listen for thoughts that sound like an excuse or a "reason" for any of your circumstances.

Decide what part you own. Maybe someone else truly didn't deliver, and you need their input to move something forward. You still have something to own. What is it? Decide what you *do* have control over. The other person is accountable for their failure, but you own a piece, too.

Don't flip from blaming others to blaming yourself. That's not an improvement! Owning up to a mistake may result in guilt, but when guilt is excessive, it is more likely a reflection of low self-esteem or manipulation. Accountability is about acknowledging, apologizing, and amending—the triple-A approach. Own the mistake, express genuine regret for your part in it, and then work on fixing it. Doing all three actions consistently and appropriately will boost your self-esteem.

Compare these two perspectives on power:

- Blaming conveys power *in the moment*, but that power is fragile; it relies on continued blaming and keeps problems from being resolved.
- Authenticity builds *power over the long view* and results in credibility, respect, and solutions.

How can you build your power and credibility over time through authentic accountability?

Be *courageously* accountable. The righteousness we feel when we blame someone else is the easy way out. Powerful leaders own up to their mistakes. Doing so paves the way for others and helps you shift from a costly blaming culture to a just and accountable one.

CHAPTER 11

Push Yourself

ONE OF THE few assumptions a person can safely make is that there is always more to learn. Never stop. This section nudges you to consider ways to broaden the scope of your leadership beyond today.

SELF-ASSESSMENT SCORING:

   1—I am struggling with or not yet skilled at this.

   2—I am starting to work on improving at this, but I need more skill building.

   3—I am making some consistent progress in improving at this.

   4—I am doing very well in this area.

Determine your current level of skill on these "push yourself" competencies (score 1–4):

   1.   I pursue new goals and do not rely on older accomplishments to maintain my sense of achievement. Score: _____

2. I have a strong sense of when to take risks and when to play it safe with growth opportunities for me or my organization, and my track record bears this out. Score: _____

3. I maintain a healthy self-confidence and use strategies to rebuild it when things happen that throw me off. Score: _____

4. I can articulate the qualities of leaders I admire and why, where I want to be in ten years, and how I want to be remembered as a leader. Score: _____

5. I practice the skill of anticipating to strategically prepare for a better future and to avoid getting stuck in a rut of "the way we've always done it." Score: _____

Now explore the corresponding sections that follow to learn how to improve skills that need work or enhance your current skills.

1. RESTING ON YOUR LAURELS

Do you lay claim to accomplishments that reflect your past performance more than your current efforts? This section helps you assess whether it might be time to pursue a new challenge and suggests actions you can take beyond simply setting a goal.

In ancient Greece, a crown of laurel leaves was worn as a symbol of victory. Today you might see universities using laurels to signify a commencement. It is right and good to acknowledge achievements! It can be satisfying—even joyful—to bask in the glow of your accomplishments. But when we wear the crown a little too long, we are "resting on our laurels," and complacency can set in.

It happens to most of us at one time or another. You may be resting on your laurels if you are in any of these situations:

- You claim talent or achievement that you are no longer actively working on.
- You feel as if you are stuck in a rut at work.
- You experience work as if there is no "movement" in your progress.
- You make statements about your area of expertise based on practices that you haven't researched for a while.
- You feel sheepish for saying that you are accomplished at something you have not kept up with. (Yes, I did earn a black belt in Tae Kwon Do, but I haven't practiced since about 1998!)
- You think your best work is behind you.

When we do something well, it is tempting to rest on our laurels. After all, we achieved something great; why not just hang out there for a while?

As with most things, we have to strike a balance. The flip side of resting on our laurels is neglecting to celebrate success at all. We jump immediately to the next project without taking time to recognize ourselves or others for a great result, and we miss the opportunity for a rush of motivation. But resting on our past accomplishments is also a problem. When we achieve something great, we raise the bar for ourselves, and that is where excellence is born.

Stay curious, especially about things you already know.
Catch yourself making strong statements about your profession or things you know *for sure*. Are you staying open to new ideas? How do you keep current with the latest research? Encourage others to challenge your thinking by asking "what if" and being the devil's advocate.

Leaders go first. One of our dogs, on our walks, loved to go around the corner ahead of us when she was off leash. We tried to train her not to do this, but she couldn't help herself. We liked to think that she *believed* she was a leader. Leaders want to see what is around the corner before anyone else, brave new trails, and pave the way for others. Do you take the time to look around the corner before others do? What changes are in store for your profession, and how can you anticipate them proactively? Begin your work week with the question "What are we doing that has gone unexamined?" Then examine it.

You know who loves you, but who doesn't? Many years ago, as part of a 360 review of my performance, I sent out questionnaires to my direct reports and colleagues. I got great reviews—talk about an invitation to rest on my laurels. Because I felt safe doing so (and I knew it would not affect my paycheck), on the next round of 360s, I expanded my request for feedback to those I knew were not as happy with my leadership. As I predicted, my scores went down, but as a result of that feedback, I changed my approach to meet the needs of a more diverse group of reviewers.

What have you read this year? We know that leading and learning is not a task to be crossed off a to-do list, but it can be easy to feel as if we've studied enough for a while. Start a book club with other leaders in your organization. Read something that doesn't confirm what you already know but rather pushes you to see something in a new light.

"Sing with singers who are better than you." It can be humbling *and* motivating to surround ourselves with people who have more talent, knowledge, and experience than we do. When I sing with singers who are better than me, I work harder and learn more. I push myself in ways that I don't when I am one of the best in the group—singing or otherwise. I used to wear a button showing someone in a contorted posture with a fitting caption: "Get behind yourself and push!"

2. CALCULATED RISKS

How do you know whether a risk is worth taking? Would others say that you are bold and daring, or that you play it too safe? This section offers questions that will help you examine your risk tolerance and your approach to managing risk.

The end of the year is a good time to ask yourself, "What risks have I taken this year?" When did you "go big or stay home?" When did you strive to act boldly and courageously, moving your team or organization forward? Don't wait for the calendar to turn. Do this reflection any time of year when you want to grow.

If I were interviewing candidates for a high-level leadership position, I would ask these questions:

- What is the last big risk you took in your work, and what was the impact on your organization's mission? (I would be looking for courage: Can they feel the fear and still act? Do they take calculated, strategic, and mission-driven risk—not just risk for the sake of taking a risk?)
- What risks did you choose not to take, and what was the impact of those choices? (Does the candidate weigh costs and benefits and understand that not all risks are worth taking? Does the candidate play it too safe?)
- What innovations do you foresee in your field of expertise in the next three to five years? What things are you doing now that may go by the wayside? (Can the candidate think strategically, beyond the day to day, and is it obvious that they have developed a practice of making time to do so?)

Beyond individual decisions on risk taking, I would ask:

- Tell me about a time when you had to convince others to take bold action when they did not think your idea would work. How did you get them to buy in? (I want to know if they have what it takes to move from individual vision to engaging others to help make it happen. Additionally, I am interested in whether they are working under an outdated hero model of leadership, or whether they really grasp that no one can do it alone.)

Walt Disney's first animated feature film, *Snow White and the Seven Dwarfs*, ended up being a timeless movie and a monumental financial success. But during production, it looked like it might all fall apart. The film ran out of money well before completion. Disney had to get people to risk putting their money into what, at the time, represented a huge change (Lambert 2019). Being a visionary doesn't do a lot of good if you can't get others to invest in you, whatever form that investment takes.

Learning how to take calculated risks comes with practice in making deliberate and thoughtful decisions, reflecting on good and bad outcomes, and incorporating lessons learned into plans for what could be better next time around. Balance that thoughtfulness and reflection with the notion that impatience—in the right circumstances—might be a virtue after all. Impatience with the status quo, with a lack of progress, with waiting until all the ducks are in a row . . . leaders who are a little impatient can help motivate bold movement. If you have a regular practice of thinking strategically, you'll be better prepared to seize opportunities when they come up.

In considering risky decisions, ask yourself these questions:

Why? What is my goal in taking this risk? Be as clear as possible. This is the opposite of acting impulsively or rashly. What is your goal worth—to you and to your organization?

Where is the power? Think about the support you might have or obtain, especially in your preparation process. Consider who has the social, financial, or other kinds of capital you need and enlist them.

What is at stake? What are you risking? Knowing your priority values is a great starting point because they can guide your decisions. Ask yourself, what will taking this risk, even if it fails, mean ten minutes from now? Ten days? Ten weeks, months, or years?

When? Is the building on fire? Then you must act immediately. With most business decisions, though, you have time to think things through. Your results will benefit from that thoughtful reflection.

3. I HAVE CONFIDENCE

> *Do* **you have confidence?** This section offers strategies to build confidence or get it back if it has suffered.

My two-year-old granddaughter, looking up while walking and unexpectedly seeing herself in a mirror, exclaimed with delight, "Oh! Me!" It is fun to watch children, with their self-centered view of the world, experience joy in just being themselves. In contrast, while I was facilitating a leadership workshop, participants walking into the room had to pass a huge mirror in the doorway and couldn't escape looking at themselves. Reflecting on what they saw without a child's enthusiasm raised the question: What happens over the years that leaves confidence tentative, intermittent at best, even for leaders?

Some of it is a natural evolution from self-centered to other-centered, learning humility as we experience a mix of success and failure. While confidence is not a static state, some ride the waves with more drastic dips than others.

Believe! Psychologist Albert Bandura (2017) coined the term "self-efficacy" to refer to the belief that you can influence the way events in your life impact you. People with high self-efficacy believe they will overcome whatever challenges arise. This belief structure is the foundation of self-confidence. The good news is that beliefs don't have to be true. We just need to choose to believe them, and we can change our beliefs. Think of someone who demonstrates the confidence you would like to have. Applying that image to yourself, what if you more consistently believed in your own success?

- **Picture it.** How would you stand differently? How would your facial expression change? When others look at you, how would they describe what they see? Look for an opportunity to physically step into this posture and experience what it is like.

- **Imagine feeling this way.** How would it feel to wholeheartedly believe that you have the ability to succeed? How would that feel different from the times you doubt yourself and your abilities? What kind of energy would be freed up if self-doubt did not weigh you down? Sit with this for a few minutes to experience the emotional state of confidence.

- **Conjure up the words.** What would you say to yourself and others if you were confident? What would you stop saying to yourself and others when your confidence is low? Tune in to specific phrases that you would like to readily call to mind.

Make a list of your accomplishments. Instead of immediately starting the next project, take note at the end of the day or week what you have achieved. Include your team—it's uplifting to everyone. Your inner nag may ask, "But what about the things you did not get done?" Silence this voice by taking one small action every day toward something that you have been putting off because you lack confidence. Avoiding accountability weakens confidence: Walk toward a challenge instead of away from it. It helps to break down challenges into small steps.

Make your mistakes work for you. Identify what you learned from your mistakes. Facilitate a discussion among your peers: "What is one of the biggest mistakes you have made in your career, and what did you learn from it that sticks with you today?" Peer support puts your mistakes into perspective and reduces the gap between how you see yourself and how you see others who you perceive as more successful.

Change the story. Emotions come from the story that accompanies an experience (much like the development of a conflict). Consider this pattern:

- Observe something (such as someone speaking before you in a meeting who does a great job).
- Tell a story in your head about it that you believe to be true (this person is a great speaker, I could never do that well, why did I ever agree to speak, I am going to fail, etc.).
- Respond to the story with an emotion (fear, sweaty palms, stomachache, dread).
- Act on that emotion (hide, speak too quietly, perform like there are concrete blocks hanging from your brain, and then beat yourself up during and after).

Instead, create a new and improved story:

- Observe something (someone speaking before you in a meeting who does a great job).
- Tell a story in your head about it that you believe to be true (I can learn from great speakers like this, I will do my best, I have things to share that the audience can relate to and benefit from).

- Respond to the story with an emotion (calm, openness, compassion, nervousness but also excitement).
- Act on that emotion (breathe deeply, speak up, look at the people you are speaking to, acknowledge the first speaker, smile).

4. LEADER LISTS

What kind of leader do you strive to be? This section helps you sort that out by prompting you to make lists of strengths, actions, role models, and so on, that define you as a leader.

Noticing our current actions reveals what is getting us closer to—*or steering us away from*—becoming the leader we strive to be. Take a few minutes to fill in the following short lists to reconnect with what leadership means for you.

- **Name three people whose leadership you admire.** Write down their names and a word or short phrase that describes what you admire most about them. Where do their influences show up in your actions? For me, my mom was eternally patient. I am not. When I'm feeling and acting impatient, I call her to mind, visualize her demeanor, and hear her voice. I remember times I paused and chose to "act" patient, and it had a soothing impact on me and others around me.
- **Name three people who respect your leadership.** Write down their names and a word that they would use to describe why they look up to you. Try to recall specific instances when your leadership was respected and enjoy for a moment the positive impact you have made.
- **Add three words or short phrases that you would use to describe your leadership strengths.** Can you recall

specific instances when you showed these strengths? What successes have you had when maximizing these strengths?

- **Choose one word that you'd like to describe you but doesn't yet.** What is one action that you could take to build this strength?

- **Name three leaders who taught you how *not* to be.** Think back on those "teachers" and write down the things you would do differently, having learned what doesn't work.

- **Add three words or phrases that your *current* team or colleagues would use to describe how they remember your leadership 20 years from now.** If they are not the words you would have hoped for, what would you rather have them say? What actions can you take to change the course of that future conversation?

5. THINKING LIKE A STRATEGIST

Does your day-to-day agenda drive the way you think? Would you like to be more strategic in your approach, but you're not sure where to start? This section offers straightforward techniques to move toward a broader way of thinking.

Strategic planning is important, but an annual event is not going to bear fruit if you don't develop the skill and habit of anticipating. How can you think more like a futurist and lift your head up above the gnarly problems of the moment that can trap you in a reactive mode?

Question the way it is. Appoint someone on your leadership team to be the weekly challenger of the status quo. "Why do we do it this way? What would happen if we tried ___ instead? We are good, but our competition is better. What do they have that we are missing? How does our process impact the patient or customer?" Taking turns in this role keeps this skill top of mind for everyone, and it prevents the questioner from being dismissed as negative or provocative.

Compare and contrast seemingly unrelated situations. Identify a success, such as recent increase in market share, improved patient satisfaction or quality numbers, etc. Pick it apart by creating a list of things that helped make it a win. Next, identify a failure, such as increasing staff turnover, higher medication errors, or a stalled project. Dissect it similarly, without blame, to explore what went wrong. Compare the two lists, which may not have any obvious connections to each other. Ask, "Where do these two diverse situations intersect? What lessons can we apply to our future work to be more ready for potential challenges?"

Get out of your zone. Talk—and listen—to people who work in different areas than you. You don't have to cross-train to do their work; just stay curious about the challenges they are facing. Picture yourself: You are in an interdepartmental meeting in which others' updates are a tempting moment to check your phone for your "real" work. Resist the temptation. In many lists of desired leadership qualities, strategic thinking tops technical skill. By listening intentionally to the priorities of others, you may discover common themes and shared concerns from which solutions can arise. Push yourself to be a contributing member to a team beyond your area of expertise.

Look at your mission and vision statements. For five minutes, think about how your actions are helping to achieve the organization's mission and vision. Start off a team meeting by asking, "What are we focused on this week that is helping to achieve our vision?" When you see someone taking action, start a dialogue: "How do you think this (action/ project) will impact our organization's mission and vision in the future?"

Make strategic thinking a habit. Start with 15 minutes a week, and put it on your calendar to ask yourself some questions. Here are some to get you started:

- Who is doing what I do better than I am? How are they doing that?
- What challenges are my colleagues in other departments facing? Where do their challenges intersect with those of my department?
- What did I learn last week? How am I communicating that with others?
- What challenge can I anticipate in the next week or month? What could I do, or encourage my team to do, that would be proactive rather than reactive?
- Is the team spending its time and energy in a way that puts us on track to reach our goals a year from now?

Asking questions that probe where you want to be next year implies that you have identified your destination. That's where strategic *planning* fits in. Strategic thinking and planning go hand in hand.

Conclusion

THE CONTENT OF this book was written over a period of ten years, but it was bound between front and back covers during the COVID-19 pandemic. The faces of leadership have changed, too, over this decade, as baby boomers have retired and a new generation of leaders with different life experiences have stepped into that space. While we can—and must—prepare for some changes, many are unpredictable. I'll leave you with three truths that I believe you can depend upon and my hopes for you:

1. **Leadership matters.** Since the beginning of time, people have looked for leaders to guide, direct, and inspire hope in the promise of a better future. *I hope you find in this book a recognition of yourself as someone who is needed, maybe now more than ever.*

2. **Whether with commitment or reluctance, with a title or without, you are already leading.** Can you lead 10 percent better today? Sometimes I listen to sleep meditations to calm my busy mind at bedtime. One of the recordings that I especially like asks something like, "Could you become just 10 percent more comfortable in whatever position you are in?" This is brilliant. I can't go from racing mind to Zen calm in a few minutes, but I can do 10 percent more. Becoming a great leader is like that, too; it comes in increments. *I hope you find in this*

book many opportunities to make progress through small adjustments.

3.   **"It's all about the journey" turns out to be more than a platitude.** I confess that I have found this often-used phrase trite, but it turns out to be a great metaphor for letting go of perfectionism. There is little room in great leadership for perfection, and I urge you to give it less mental and emotional space. A journey starts with a destination in mind, a map of how to get there, a pack loaded with the supplies you need, and the promise of adventure. But journeys can take unexpected turns and rarely go as perfectly as planned. We may lose our passport, our umbrella, our way, our enthusiasm. What then? Make the best of it. Adapt and find adventure when you are in the mess of things. It's either that or suffering— which is a legitimate choice, but keep in mind that it is a choice. *I hope you find in this book just the message you need, at the time you need it, to navigate the bumps in your path as you journey forward.*

Thank you for joining me here.
Ever onward.

References

Babauta, L. 2017. "A Guide to Cultivating Compassion in Your Life, with 7 Practices." *Zen Habits*. Published June 4. http://zenhabits.net/a-guide-to-cultivating-compassion-in-your-life-with-7-practices/.

Bandura, A. 2017. "Self-Efficacy." Accessed September 2, 2020. https://albertbandura.com/albert-bandura-self-efficacy.html.

Baron-Cohen, S. 2020. "Reading the Mind in the Eyes Test." University of Cambridge. Accessed March 26. http://socialintelligence.labinthewild.org/mite/.

Bradberry, T. 2015. "10 Toxic People You Should Avoid at All Costs." *Forbes*. Published November 10. www.forbes.com/sites/travisbradberry/2015/11/10/10-toxic-people-you-should-avoid-at-all-costs/.

Bratt, M. 2009. "Retaining the Next Generation of Nurses: The Wisconsin Nurse Residency Program Provides a Continuum of Support." *Journal of Continuing Education in Nursing* 40 (9): 416–25.

Bregman, P. 2011. *18 Minutes: Find Your Focus, Master Distraction, and Get the Right Things Done*. New York: Business Plus.

Buckingham, M. 2005. *The One Thing You Need to Know . . . About Great Managing, Great Leading and Sustained Individual Success*. New York: Free Press.

Cain, S. 2012. "The Power of Introverts." TED Talk. Published February 2012. www.ted.com/talks/susan_cain_the_power_of_introverts.

Duhigg, C. 2016. "What Google Learned from Its Quest to Build the Perfect Team." *New York Times Magazine*. Published February 28. www.nytimes.com/2016/02/28/magazine/what-google-learned-from-its-quest-to-build-the-perfect-team.html.

Espinoza, C., M. Ukleja, and C. Rusch. 2010. *Managing the Millennials: Discover the Core Competencies for Managing Today's Workforce*. Hoboken, NJ: John Wiley & Sons.

Frederickson, B. 2009. *Positivity*. New York: Harmony Books.

French, J. R. P., and B. Raven. 1959. "The Bases of Social Power." *Classics of Organization Theory* 7: 311–20.

Goldsmith, M., with M. Reiter. 2007. *What Got You Here Won't Get You There*. New York: Hyperion.

Gordon, J. 2017. "Know Your Why: What Is Your Purpose?" *Jon Gordon's Weekly Newsletter*. Published July 10. www.jongordon.com/positivetip/know-your-why.html.

Greenleaf Center for Servant Leadership. 2020. "What Is Servant Leadership?" Accessed August 19. www.greenleaf.org/what-is-servant-leadership/.

Grice, A. 2012. "Nick Clegg: I'm Not Sorry for Saying I'm Sorry." *The Independent*. Published September 22. www.independent.co.uk/news/uk/politics/nick-clegg-im-not-sorry-for-saying-im-sorry-8163879.html.

Gundersen Health System. 2015. "Gundersen Reaches First Days of Energy Independence." Published November 10. www.gundersenhealth.org/our-system/news/2015/gundersen-reaches-first-days-of-energy-independence/.

Gurel, E. 2017. "SWOT Analysis: A Theoretical Review." *Journal of International Social Research* 10: 994–1006.

Habitat for Humanity International. 2020. "Our Mission, Vision, and Principles." Accessed September 2. www.habitat.org/about/mission-and-vision.

Harvard Business School. 2016. "The Failed Launch of www.healthcare.gov." Published November 18. https://digital.hbs.edu/platform-rctom/submission/the-failed-launch-of-www-healthcare-gov/.

Heath, C., and D. Heath. 2010. *Switch: How to Change Things When Change Is Hard*. New York: Crown.

Heiser, S. 2017. "More Women than Men Enrolled in U.S. Medical Schools in 2017." Association of American Medical Colleges. Published December 17. www.aamc.org/news-insights/press-releases/more-women-men-enrolled-us-medical-schools-2017.

Lambert, R. 2019. "Disney's Snow White: The Risk That Changed Filmmaking Forever." Published February 8. www.denofgeek.com/movies/disneys-snow-white-the-risk-that-changed-filmmaking-forever/.

Loehr, J., and T. Schwartz. 2003. *The Power of Full Engagement: Managing Energy, Not Time, Is the Key to High Performance and Personal Renewal*. New York: Free Press.

Machovina, J. 2014. "Bring Your Webcast A-Game." Presentation at the Southwest Wisconsin Association for Training and Development Workshop, November 6.

Mann, A. 2018. "Why We Need Best Friends at Work." Gallup. Published January 15. www.gallup.com/workplace/236213/why-need-best-friends-work.aspx.

May, R. 1994. *The Courage to Create*. New York: W. W. Norton.

McArdle, A., J. Ali, and N. Brown. 2007. "Hand Hygiene and Healthcare Associated Infections." *BMJ* 334 (Suppl. S6): 0706220.

Medina, J. 2008. *Brain Rules: 12 Principles for Surviving and Thriving at Work, Home and School*. Seattle, WA: Pear Press.

Myers, D. 2015. "Are All Minnesotans Above Average?" *Science Friday*. Published November 6. www.sciencefriday.com/segments/are-all-minnesotans-above-average/

Peck, S. 1978. *The Road Less Traveled: A New Psychology of Love, Traditional Values and Spiritual Growth*. New York: Touchstone.

Pew Research Center. 2015. "U.S. Public Becoming Less Religious." Published November 3. www.pewforum.org/2015/11/03/u-s-public-becoming-less-religious/.

Pink, D. 2009. *Drive: The Surprising Truth About What Motivates Us*. New York: Riverhead Books.

Rath, T. 2007. *Strengths Finders 2.0*. New York: Gallup Press.

Robertson, L. 1984. *Laurel's Kitchen Bread Book*. New York: Random House.

Ross, H. 2014. "Everyday Bias: Further Explorations into How the Unconscious Mind Shapes Our World at Work." Cook Ross. Accessed August 26, 2020. www.cookross.com/docs/everyday_bias.pdf.

Rural Wisconsin Health Cooperative (RWHC). 2020. "Rural Wisconsin Communities Will Be the Healthiest in the Nation." Published April. www.rwhc.com/AboutUs/Vision,MissionStrategicPriorities.aspx.

Sadker, D., M. Sadker, and K. Zittleman. 2009. *Still Failing at Fairness: How Gender Bias Cheats Girls and Boys in School and What We Can Do About It*. New York: Scribner.

Schoenholz, P. I., and C. A. Burkhart-Kriesel. 2008. "Fist to Five." In *Working with Groups: Generating Ideas, Making Decisions, and Enhancing Communication*. Lincoln: University of Nebraska.

Senge, P. 1990. *The Fifth Discipline*. New York: Doubleday.

Stafford, A. 2012. "My Mother's Peasant Bread." *Alexandra Cooks*. Published November 7. https://alexandracooks.com/2012/11/07/my-mothers-peasant-bread-the-best-easiest-bread-you-will-ever-make/.

Tanenbaum. 2020. "Tanenbaum Diversity Checklist." Accessed August 26. https://tanenbaum.org/programs/workplace/workplace-resources/religious-diversity-checklist/.

U.S. Census Bureau. 2013. "Male Nurses Becoming More Commonplace." Published February 25. www.census.gov/newsroom/press-releases/2013/cb13-32.html.

Weeks, L. 2010. "Impatient Nation: I Can't Wait for You to Read This." National Public Radio. Published December 10. www.npr.org/2010/12/06/131565694/impatient-nation-i-can-t-wait-for-you-to-read-this.

Wing Sue, D. 2010. *Microaggressions in Everyday Life: Race, Gender, and Sexual Orientation*. Hoboken, NJ: John Wiley & Sons.

————. 2003. *Overcoming our Racism: The Journey to Liberation*. San Francisco: Jossey-Bass.

Ziff, D. 2010. "MATC President Tries to Sell Public on $133.8 Million Building Expansion." *Wisconsin State Journal*. October 19. https://madison.com/wsj/news/local/govt-and-politics/elections/matc-president-tries-to-sell-public-on-133-8-million-building-expansion/article_b1eb576c-d8ad-11df-8b23-001cc4c002e0.html.

Additional Resources

Bariso, J. 2019. "I Just Discovered Warren Buffet's 25-5 Rule: Completely Brilliant." *Inc.* Published September 9. www.inc.com/justin-bariso/i-just-discovered-warren-buffets-25-5-rule-completely-brilliant.html.

Brown, B. 2018. *Dare to Lead*. New York: Random House.

Kotter, J. 2012. *Leading Change*. Boston: Harvard Business Review Press.

McCarthy, N. 2017. "American Workers Get the Short End on Vacation Days." *Forbes*. Published June 26. www.forbes.com/sites/niallmccarthy/2017/06/26/american-workers-have-a-miserable-vacation-allowance-infographic/.

Patterson, K., J. Grenny, R. McMillan, and A. Switzler, A. 2012. *Crucial Conversations: Tools for Talking When the Stakes Are High*. New York: McGraw-Hill.

Peterson, C., and M. Seligman. 2005. "VIA Survey of Character Strengths." Accessed September 2, 2020. https://ppc.sas.upenn.edu/resources/questionnaires-researchers/survey-character-strengths.

Portney, S. 2010. *Project Management for Dummies*, 3rd ed. Hoboken, NJ: John Wiley & Sons.

Ruiz, M. 1997. *The Four Agreements: A Practical Guide to Personal Freedom*. San Rafael, CA: Amber-Allen Publishing.

Wakeman, C. 2017. *No Ego: How Leaders Can Cut the Cost of Workplace Drama, End Entitlement, and Drive Big Results*. New York: St. Martin's Press.

Whitelaw, G. 2012. *The Zen Leader: 10 Ways to Go from Barely Managing to Leading Fearlessly*. Pompton Plains, NJ: Career Press.

About the Author

Jo Anne Preston is the Workforce and Organizational Development Senior Manager for the Rural Wisconsin Health Cooperative (RWHC). RWHC serves rural hospitals in Wisconsin with a variety of products and services to support and enhance rural healthcare. In her role at RWHC, Jo Anne focuses on both workforce development (serving on collaborative task forces to secure the healthcare workforce of the future) and leadership development (developing and teaching leadership workshops focused on the unique needs of rural healthcare leaders).

Since 1981, Jo Anne has honed her leadership skills in rural healthcare. She worked for 20 years in substance abuse and mental health services, including a variety of middle management roles, ultimately serving as executive director for Ministry Behavioral Health in central Wisconsin. Later she worked in the Ministry Health Care corporate office in organizational development, focusing on work culture, employee engagement initiatives, and leadership development throughout the Ministry Health Care system hospitals and clinics. Her experience in leadership education and consultation has taken her across the United States to teach workshops and offer leadership coaching to new and experienced managers. She also has designed and delivered programs for healthcare organizations to enhance the patient and employee experience.

Jo Anne holds a master's degree in educational psychology and community counseling and a bachelor's degree in family services from Eastern Illinois University. She completed a certificate in

Zen Leadership from the Institute of Zen Leadership in 2019. She has written a monthly leadership newsletter since 2010, culminating in this book. Learn more about RWHC and contact Jo Anne at www.rwhc.com.